FILM BASICS AND BEYOND
Covering R/C Airplanes

by Faye Stilley

About the Author

As a 19-time award winner at the Toledo R/C Exposition, Faye Stilley has proven that iron-on covering can produce a finish that can put you in the winners' circle. He has never entered a contest without receiving an award!

Faye acquired his extraordinary skill using the "trial-and-error" method. This isn't surprising, because there are no schools for his craft–no "only way" to accomplish contest-winning results.

Although many people are willing to give advice, it's rare that anyone will explain exactly how and why he does things. Faye is an exception. You'll benefit from the many occasions he has had to tear off the covering and start again. In this book, he tells you how to get it right the first time. And he goes one step further by explaining the techniques he has developed to make an ordinary covering job into an award-winning showstopper.

President and CEO: Louis DeFrancesco Jr.
Technical Editor: Tom Atwood
Publication Manager/Copy Editor: Laura M. Kidder
Book Design: Stephanie L. Warzecha
Cover Photo: Walter Sidas
Photo Coordinator: Lisa Knorra

Contents

CHAPTER   PAGE

Introduction 6

1   Surface Preparation for Film Covering 8

2   Preparing to Cover 12

3   Covering Wings and Feathers 14

4   Covering Fuselages 18

5   Panel Lines 23

6   Stars 25

7   Scallops 27

8   Flames...31

9   Rivets and other Neat Stuff 35

10 Multicolored Trim Schemes 38

11 Maintenance and Repair 43

12 The Finishing Touches 45

13 Winners and Losers 50

    Appendix..54

Introduction

There are many different iron-on covering films available. You can use the techniques presented in this book with any of them.

All the covering techniques discussed in this book were developed using Super MonoKote, but you can use them to apply any of the many iron-on coverings on the market today. This book concentrates on how to achieve award-winning covering jobs—from preparing the surface properly through design and application of unique, unusual trim schemes. This hands-on guide to working with heat-shrink covering materials provides techniques that are all designed for one purpose—to add beauty to your airplane.

FILM CHOICE
Each film manufacturer makes its own claims about the uniqueness of its products, yet all films are similar in the sense that you apply them with heat and you can stretch and shrink them.

There are, of course, differences in depth of color, texture, shine, weight, strength, etc., and some require you to apply an adhesive to wooden surfaces before you cover them. From the standpoint of application techniques, the major difference seems to be in the amount of heat that's required to activate the adhesive and cause the material to shrink.

Once you've learned the various covering techniques, the brand of iron-on covering you choose will only be a matter of personal choice—one that can be based on such simple things as color and texture.

TO SEAL OR NOT TO SEAL
I know of only one manufacturer that strongly recommends a covering technique that I don't use. The directions that come with Oracover instruct you to iron it onto every square inch of the airframe to strengthen the structure. It seems logical that sealing the covering tightly to the wood—creating a lamination of film and wood—would increase the structural strength, and the Oracover fans among my friends have recommended this

Using the film-covering techniques in this book (along with some minor cockpit, cowling and rudder fin alterations), an Andrews Sport Master was transformed into this Messerschmitt. This plane won first place at the '82 WRAM show.

film as one of the toughest. Still, I've only used this technique once, and unless the surface is perfectly smooth, the grain of the wood and every other imperfection will show through the covering.

I have airplanes more than 10 years old that were covered without sealing the covering onto the wood (except at the seams, where different pieces of film join). In all those years of flying, the MonoKote has never come loose, and none of the airframes has failed or been fractured in the air; the structural strength was built into the airframes.

FOLLOW THE MANUFACTURER'S DIRECTIONS

It's always good to follow the manufacturer's directions. When I started to use iron-on coverings, there were no specific directions available, so I learned by trial and error. Today, manufacturers provide a page or two of hints and heat recommendations.

Rather than provide a specific temperature, some manufacturers suggest heat estimates such as "about 300 degrees Fahrenheit." Others cite ranges such as "250 to 300 degrees Fahrenheit." In my

This Twin-Twin took third place in MonoKote and second place in Sport Monoplane at the '92 Toledo show. More of this plane's covering details are shown in Chapter 13, "Winners and Losers."

This Unitaar was "kit-bashed" from a Pacific Aire Showbird. It was covered using MonoKote, and it features hundreds of flush rivets. (It won first place at the '83 WRAM show.)

experience, the exact temperature of the iron isn't critical. If it were, we would all be in trouble because the heat irons available to us can't maintain an exact temperature. They all drift, somewhat, over a range of temperatures.

When you consider a heat gun's heat output, the actual temperature applied to the surface varies all over the place. The underlying surface (wood or air), the distance you hold the gun from that surface and how long you hold it there all affect the actual heat that's being applied.

FIND THE BEST TEMPERATURES

The amount of heat that you use must be important because everyone talks about it. It's important but not critical. Only the low- and high-temperature tolerances of a particular covering are critical. If you don't use enough heat, the adhesive won't stick; if you use too much, you'll burn a hole in the covering or melt it.

The correct amount of heat will be determined by the covering's characteristics and how you handle it and your heating tools. As you work within the low and high tolerances of the covering you've chosen, you'll find the temperatures that work best. The correct amount of heat is that which allows you to accomplish what you're trying to do. For instance, when you apply trim, you'll want enough heat to make a good bond, but not so much as to cause bubbles or wrinkles. Although the correct amount will be in the low to mid range, you'll come into the equation owing to the amount of pressure you exert with the iron. You'll also enter the equation when you cover a curved surface such as a wing tip, because the harder you pull the covering, the less heat you'll need—and vice versa.

In summary, you're the main ingredient in accomplishing an outstanding covering job. The techniques that you use and the skill with which you use them will make the difference.

1

Surface Preparation for Film Covering

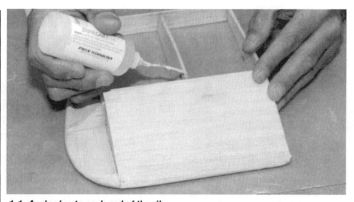

1-1. Apply glue to each end of the rib.

If you plan to use a heat-sensitive plastic covering on your model, the first thing to consider is the surface over which it will be stretched. Unlike paint, which is much more forgiving because fillers and multiple coats hide surface imperfections, plastic film shows virtually every rough spot. Film isn't much thicker than a fancy

ing is plain, smooth wood. Even the slightest bit of glue on the wood will grab the film, and cause high spots, low spots and pulls.

Film covering should be stretched tautly over the wood, but not heat-sealed to it. This will help to eliminate bubbling and wrinkling. Except for where two pieces of film join along a seam, there's no reason to seal the covering to the wood.

AVOID GLUE ON THE SURFACE

It's very important to keep glue away from the outside surface. There will be many opportunities to put glue on a piece of wood that will eventually become part of the outside surface. Don't do it! Impossible, you say? Perhaps. But avoid it like the plague! Think "covering" right from the beginning of the project, and remember to glue from the inside. To help you keep glue away from the wood's outside surface, I offer the following suggestions for those areas where it's especially tempting to take thin CA and pour it on.

• **Capstrips.** Apply thick CA on the rib at both ends, and then put the capstrip across the rib and hold it until the CA sets. When the capstrips are in place, turn the wing over

1-2. Hold the capstrip at each end until it sets.

1-3. Use thin CA on the underside of the capstrip.

1-4. When applying CA to a wing-tip block, allow about 1/4 inch clearance around the outside edge.

paint job, and there are advantages to using it. It weighs less and isn't as messy as paint, and even a beginner can achieve results that look better than most paint jobs. The best surface to use for cover-

and finish gluing them in place from the underside with thin CA. (See Photos 1-1 to 1-3.) The surface to be covered will be glue-free.

• **Leading- and trailing-edge sheeting.** The leading edge is particularly important because you're building a laminated surface. The top and bottom sheeting is glued to both sides of the leading edge. Glued laminates always have some glue on their edges. The problem is compounded with the leading edge, because you'll be shaping the laminate and, therefore, feathering the glue, i.e., giving it an even greater surface area.

Shape the top and bottom of the leading-edge stock to a flat surface angle that extends the forward contour of the rib top and bottom. (See Figure A.) Don't round the stock. The flatter the stock's surface, the tighter the sheeting

1-5. When you butt together two pieces of balsa, run a small bead of glue down the center of the edges.

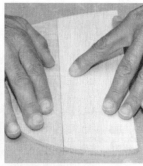

1-6. Carefully butt the pieces together on a piece of wax paper, and hold them until the glue sets.

1-7. Removing a glob of CA from a piece of balsa is easier than you may think.

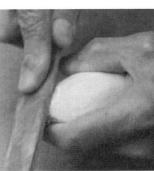

1-8. An ordinary file removes CA without damaging the balsa.

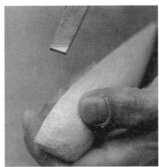

1-9. The CA has been removed and only a stain in the wood remains. Sanding and polishing will recover the smooth surface that existed before the spill.

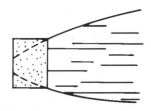

Figure A
Shape the top and bottom of the leading-edge stock to a flat surface that continues the forward contour of the rib top and bottom.

Figure B
Tape the sheeting as tightly as possible to the flattened stock, and glue it to the spar from the back.

will fit, thereby minimizing the glue that's exposed to the surface.

First, place the sheeting on the leading edge. Don't pin it, except for position. Tape the sheeting as tightly as possible to the leading-edge stock (Figure B), and glue from the back with thick CA. Keep pressure on the CA by rubbing your finger across the top surface of the sheeting on the leading edge. Glue only the spar and the sheeting.

Once the sheeting has set on the leading edge, gently bend the sheeting away from the ribs, and put a bead of thick CA on each rib. In tight places, tip the wing upward, and allow the CA to run down the rib edge to the leading edge. Pull the sheeting back, and press firmly with your hands with a brushing action toward the back of the wing. This technique ensures that all the glue will be inside the structure.

• **Wing-tip blocks.** Hardened surface glue at this critical point will grab the covering and prevent it from shrinking properly over the wing tip. There's usually too much covering at the wing tip and, to avoid wrinkles, it must be shrunk as it's laid over the tip's surface and sealed to it. Therefore, you must apply the glue carefully. Use thick CA on the tip block, and allow about $1/4$ inch clearance all the way around the outer edge. (See Photo 1-4.) When you press the tip block into place, the glue will be spread onto the bare wood area, and very little, if any, will be squeezed out to the surface.

• **Solid balsa fins, rudders and stabilizers.** When two pieces of balsa are butted together to form a larger piece, carefully run a small bead of glue down the center of the edges to be joined. On a flat surface that's protected with wax paper or film wrap, butt the two edges together, and hold them

firmly until they set. (See Photos 1-5 and 1-6.) Only a little glue should be squeezed onto the surface. Remember, to keep surfaces glue-free, think "glue inside."

1-10. Covering small parts first is easier than gluing the model together and then trying to cover it!

REMOVING SURFACE GLUE
What can be done when the inevitable happens and a glob of epoxy gets on the outside, or some thin CA sneaks through a joint?

If it's a major accident, it's better to replace the piece of wood than to try and clean it. Fortunately, with a little patience, you can soften and remove many CA spills using CA debonder—a product offered under various brand names. If a dent or a hole remains, you can correct it with filler.

If you do get a glob of CA on the outside surface, the best way to

1-11. These are the tools I recommend for shaping, sanding and polishing. They include a variety of sanding blocks, files and rasps, sandpaper cleaner and a tack cloth.

1-12. My favorite tool for rough shaping is a rasp.

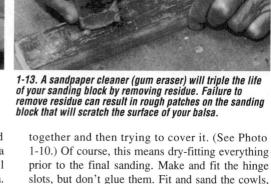

1-13. A sandpaper cleaner (gum eraser) will triple the life of your sanding block by removing residue. Failure to remove residue can result in rough patches on the sanding block that will scratch the surface of your balsa.

remove it is with a metal file. (See Photos 1-7 and 1-8.) Sandpaper will just dig a trough into the balsa around the hardened CA, but a metal file will remove the CA with minimal damage to the balsa. After you've filed the glue away, use a sanding block to finish the surface. The balsa will be slightly discolored from the CA residue that soaked into the wood, but the surface will be clean. (See Photo 1-9.)

Epoxy is a sticky mess before it sets. After removing the epoxy by carefully wiping it off the surface, clean the grain by wiping the wood with a cloth that has been soaked in alcohol or acetone. This will also thin any remaining epoxy and allow it to sink into the wood.

COVERING SMALL PARTS

Continue to think "covering" while you build, and keep in mind that covering small, uncomplicated parts is much easier than gluing the whole thing

together and then trying to cover it. (See Photo 1-10.) Of course, this means dry-fitting everything prior to the final sanding. Make and fit the hinge slots, but don't glue them. Fit and sand the cowls, but remove them for covering. Cover any part that can be done separately, and glue it into place later. This minimizes the risk of damaging an already covered area when you handle your model to cover a complicated area.

FILLING AND SANDING

Before you start to cover, the balsa surfaces should almost shine. You must fill all the dings and pinholes with a lightweight balsa filler. (Several brands are available.) When the filler has dried, remove as much of the wood's grain as possible. Of course, the grain can't be eliminated completely, and the color will remain. The objective is to flatten the grain so that the harder and softer areas have a uniform surface.

Don't be tempted to "palm-sand." Soft grain is eaten away more quickly than hard grain, and you'll therefore be accentuating the grain that you're trying to eliminate.

SANDING BLOCKS

Always use a block for sanding. Several sizes will come in handy, e.g., large ones are good for wings and other flat surfaces, but small sanding blocks can ruin what's supposed to be a flat surface. Different-size dowels that are covered with sandpaper also come in handy for curved surfaces, such as fillets. These surfaces must be carefully sanded, because you'll be sealing the covering to them. Blemishes here can ruin the appearance of an otherwise beautiful model.

SHAPING, SANDING AND POLISHING

To some extent, sandpaper selection is a personal choice. Use the coarser, 40- to 60-grit papers for shaping and for cutting through hard grains and adhesives. Depending on the weight of your hand, you may prefer 100- to 80-grit paper for rough sanding.

I differentiate between final shaping and rough

1-14. Lightweight filler, e.g., Carl Goldberg Models Model Magic, can be used to fill dents before covering. Shown here is a dented wing-tip block, filler, and Micro Mark tools, which I use to apply filler.

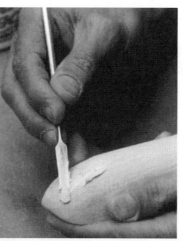

1-15. Filler is applied to the dent.

1-16. I'm using 400-grit sandpaper with a wide sanding block, which gives me excellent control.

shaping. Rough shaping is done with knives, gouges, rasps and saws. Final shaping puts the surface within $1/16$ inch of its finished shape.

Some modelers use 220-grit sandpaper to smooth the final shape to an interim finish, but my hand is a little too heavy for it, so I use 320-grit paper. The shape should be smooth but not shiny.

Once the final shaping has been accomplished, the polishing process begins. Polishing can be done with 400-, 600- and even 1,000-grit sandpaper. They all provide a finish on the wood that will "disappear" under the covering. I often jump from 320- to 600-grit sandpaper. Occasionally, on leading edges (which are always hard surfaces because of the glue/wood laminate), I use 400-grit in place of 600-grit, and then I polish with 1,000-grit. Because the covering is stretched tautly over and sealed to leading edges, wing tips and tail feathers, these areas stick out like sore thumbs unless they're really smooth. (See Photos 1-11 to 1-19.)

VACUUM BETWEEN EACH SANDING
Vacuuming the model thoroughly between each sanding will ensure that you see imperfections. (See Photo 1-20.) If you sand with your right hand, use your left hand to feel the surface for irregularities, and vice versa. The hand that does less work has the more sensitive touch.

With the final sanding (polishing) completed, it's time for another thorough vacuuming. Be particularly attentive to hinge slots and any openings to the inside of the fuselage and wings. The inside of the fuselage and wings should also be vacuumed.

TACK CLOTH
The final touch is a complete wipe-down—inside and out—with a good tack cloth. (See Photo 1-21.) A second wipe-down will catch the dust that the tack cloth disturbed but didn't pick up. This should be done as far away from your shop as possible, and these parts shouldn't be returned to the shop until they've been completely covered. No matter how clean your shop is, there will be something that can get under the covering. When your model has been covered and sealed, it's back to the shop

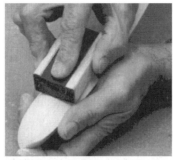

1-17. Here, I'm using a small sanding block with 600-grit sandpaper for final polishing.

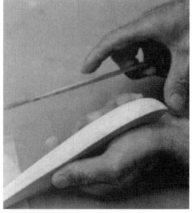

1-18. Feel the surface with the hand that's not doing all the work! It will be more sensitive.

1-19. This is the finished tip block after a CA glob has been removed and a dent has been filled. Neither will show through the plastic film after the block has been covered.

for final assembly.

Learning to cover with film covering materials can be broken down into seven steps:
1. You swear at the covering.
2. You swear at the iron.
3. You swear at yourself.
4. You talk to the covering and the iron.
5. You talk to yourself.
6. You begin to answer yourself.
7. Some kind of magic takes over. Even what seemed impossible is now working, and the only talking is being done by all the people who are admiring your work.

In the next chapter, I'll provide information that will prepare you to jump directly into Step 7.

1-20. Vacuum the model between each sanding!

1-21. The final touch is a complete wipe-down, inside and outside, with a tack cloth.

CHAPTER

2

Preparing to Cover

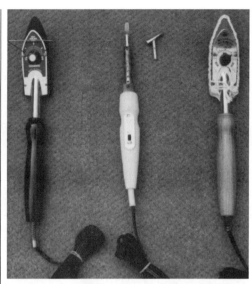

2-1. Obtain the necessary covering tools. I use three irons: two of the standard size—one set to a high temp and one to a low temp—and a smaller "trim" iron. Notice the cotton sock on the iron to the right; it will prevent the film from being scratched.

I used iron-on covering film on my first airplane and have continued to use it ever since. I like it because it's light, strong and easy to apply, and it comes in a variety of colors. It sticks to almost anything—no adhesive required—and, when sealed to itself, it forms a permanent, fuelproof bond. (Note: there are some epoxies/resins that film won't adhere to; applying Balsarite to such surfaces will ensure a good seal.) This material's unique properties allow you to shrink it and stretch it, so you can cover even the most intricate shapes. Many films change color when you apply enough heat. When they cool down, they return to their original color.

Iron-on film has a straightforward character about it, and it's very predictable. With a little experience, you'll easily be able to tell where to pull and stretch it and where to shrink it before you seal it. To guarantee successful covering, remember two important things:

• **Be patient! Don't rush!** Let the heat—not the pressure of the iron—do the work. Take your time positioning the film before you seal it. If you feel rushed or edgy, let the covering wait for a better time. You'll be glad that you did.

• **Know the characteristics of the material.** If you haven't used iron-on film before, don't experiment on your new airplane. Build an open structure, such as a portion of a wing with a tip, and use a scrap of sheet balsa about 1/4 inch thick to simulate a fin or a stab. Sacrifice a little time and film to experiment before you attack a new airframe.

2-2. A pocket thermometer, such as this one from Coverite, will help you to maintain the iron's temperature.

IRON-ON FILM HAS CHARACTER

When you apply film using high heat (for example, with MonoKote, 300 degrees Fahrenheit), several things can happen:

• The film will shrink quickly—possibly causing lightweight structures to warp. (Note: the film's ability to shrink rapidly can be useful when you want to straighten an existing warp or add washout.)

• The film will stick to wooden surfaces so tightly that if you pull it off, it will take wood with it. It's also more likely to bond to itself permanently, in which case you'll destroy it if you try to pull it apart.

• It may become "stressed," and this will cause it to wrinkle later, even though it may look fine when you first apply it.

• When you pull the film and press it with an iron, you'll seal it to the surface immediately—possibly with permanently ironed-in wrinkles.

• The film may be sealed into the grain of the wood, and this will cause the grain to show through it.

• If you hold a heat gun too close to the film for too long, you'll burn through it.

• The film will stretch more when you pull it.

• As you press the iron along seams and joints, adhesive may be squeezed from under the top layer of film. (Note: you can remove this excess glue with acetone.)

When you apply film using low heat (for example, with MonoKote, 200 to 220 degrees Fahrenheit):

• The film will shrink gradually, and it will adhere slightly, but not permanently.

• You'll be able to smooth it over solid surfaces easily—without bubbles or wrinkles.

2-3. Have rigid and flexible straightedges handy.

• Trim will be easier to apply, yet it won't be permanent, so you'll be able to reposition it if you don't get it right on the first try.

OTHER CHARACTERISTICS

Iron-on film will allow you to perform magic. There are, however, a few more characteristics that I'd like to point out so that you'll know what to expect and be able to use this knowledge to your advantage:

• You can stretch iron-on film without heat, and this enables you to tack it in place and smooth out any wrinkles before you shrink it and/or seal it.

• It's made of plastic, so it can be scratched easily.

Always seal it with heat; don't rub it excessively with the iron.

• Because film is thin, soft and flexible, pressure from your iron can put dents in the wood beneath it.

• If you remove the film's backing sheet and allow its adhesive sides to touch, they'll stick together, and you'll damage the film if you try to pull them apart.

• Although it often sticks to the backing sheet firmly, it will never stick to it permanently.

• When its adhesive is hot, the film can slip off the surface that you're covering. Be sure to hold it in place for a couple of seconds to allow it to cool.

• It will dull razor blades, modeling knives and scissors very quickly.

• The color, from roll to roll, may not be consistent. Before you buy more than one roll of the "same" color, check that they really do match. If the dealer is agreeable, take the rolls outside, and peel back a little of the plastic wrap to get a good look at the true color.

TOOLS

The proper tools can make the difference between a final product that looks like your first attempt at hanging wallpaper and one that looks like a professional paint job.

• **Irons.** Don't use a clothes iron, because adhesive will stick to it and come off on something the next time it's used for its true purpose. The weight and shape of the iron will also cause problems. Just forget it, and get the right tools.

There are many covering irons available. You'll need at least one standard-size iron and one smaller "trim" iron. Don't let the name fool you. Trim irons are absolutely indispensable for covering, not just trimming. Cotton socks are available for standard-size irons to help prevent the covering from being scratched.

Temperature is important when you apply any iron-on film. It's the dynamic that makes the stuff work. Too little or too much heat will cause many unwanted surprises. You'll need a pocket thermometer (see Photo 2-2) because covering irons don't hold their heat settings well. In addition, the numbers on the irons' dials don't have anything to do with temperature; they're only there to help you switch from off to low to high, etc.

• **Heat guns.** Several models of heat gun are on the market, and all those that I've used work well. They operate like hair dryers, but they supply a hotter stream of air, and some have a choice of nozzles. Remember that when you use a heat gun, you'll need to wear a glove on the hand that stretches or lifts the film.

• **Blades.** Dull razor or hobby-knife blades cause many problems, so be prepared to change them frequently. It's good to buy a box of 100 blades before you start a covering project. Otherwise, you'll try to stretch the life of a blade only to mess up a nice covering job and cause yourself a lot of grief.

• **Straightedges.** A good metal straightedge or ruler is a must. It's preferable to have two—one that's rigid and one that's flexible. (See Photo 2-3.) The flexible one will help you to trim the covering on curved surfaces; the rigid one will help you to cut along leading edges, etc.

• **Acetate.** A thin piece of stiff acetate will come in

2-4. Acetate is useful for cutting trim over a covered surface; transparency marking pens are also a must.

handy when you make a trim cut over a surface that has already been covered. (Two weights or thicknesses are shown in Photo 2-4.) This material is often used for making overhead-projector transparencies, and stationery stores sell it.

• **Marking pens.** You'll need permanent and water-soluble fine-line marking pens. Most regular pens won't work on plastic, so you'll need the type that's used to write on overhead-projector transparencies. All stationery stores carry them.

• **Needles.** Buy a package of sewing needles to puncture bubbles. Thin, sharp needles, like those in Photo 2-5, work the best, because they make the smallest holes. Don't use ordinary straight pins; they aren't sharp enough, and they make big holes.

• **Ironing board.** Although an ironing board that has a pad and a cover isn't necessary, it's very useful. It makes an excellent work table, and the pad protects the film from nicks and scratches. You can adjust the height of most boards, so you can sit or stand, or assume any other position in between. You'll find yourself in some strange positions because, sometimes, two hands just aren't enough. You'll probably end up using your knees, armpits, chin, stomach and a variety of other props before you finish your project.

2-5. Sewing needles are the tools for eliminating bubbles.

If you "borrow" an ironing board, buy your own cover, because you're going to get stains on it. I own my own board; it's much simpler that way.

Knowing what to expect from your covering material and having the proper tools will save you hours of work and help to keep your blood pressure down.

3

Covering Wings and Feathers

3-1. Clean the frame twice with a tack cloth.

In this chapter, I outline the process of covering wings and feathers—step by step. The first step is very important. Clean the structure—inside and out—with a tack cloth. Then go back and do it again to remove the dust that was loosened, but not picked up, the first time. (See Photo 3-1.)

Cut the film so that it's larger than the area you plan to cover. You'll need an extra 2 inches at the leading and trailing edges and the wing root and about 3 inches at the wing tip.

It's easier to cover a wing in halves (left side/right side), but you can do the whole top or bottom at once. Again, position the covering over the structure with the appropriate overlaps. Always do the bottom surface first so that the seam will be under the wing when you apply the upper covering. (See Photo 3-2.)

In the next few steps, you'll really take advantage of being able to stretch the material without using heat. First, with your iron set to a high temperature, tack the covering to the wing half. Start in the center of the leading edge and use a light touch. (See Photo 3-3.) Pull and stretch the covering to the trailing edge, and tack it in place as shown in Photo 3-4. The wrinkles to the left and right of center will be pulled out as you proceed.

Grab the covering at the leading edge of the wing root, pull it out and away from the wing, and tack it in place. (See Photo 3-5.) Then grab it at the center of the root, i.e., back from the leading edge, and tack it in place. Do the same at the root's trailing edge, and then at the wing-tip *rib,* but not at the tip piece. You'll handle that later.

At this point, most of the diagonal wrinkles will have been smoothed. Just note that some of them will remain until after you've tacked down the balance of the loose material along the

3-2. Cover the bottom of the wing first.

3-3. Tack the material at the center of the leading edge.

3-4. Pull the material back, and tack it to the trailing edge.

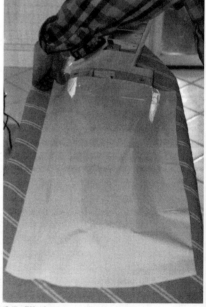

3-5. Eliminate wrinkles by pulling toward the root at the leading edge.

leading and trailing edges.

Next, grab the film at the trailing edge, halfway between the wing center and the tip rib. Pull it away from the leading edge, and then tack it into place at the trailing edge as shown in Photo 3-6. Repeat this process at the leading edge as shown in Photo 3-7.

Continue to pull out the wrinkles and tack the film along the leading and trailing edges. Tack the covering down in places that are halfway between previous "tack points." While you continue to add more and more of these points, those that you made earlier will loosen as the covering stretches and the wrinkles disappear. Partway through this process, you'll find yourself pulling out new wrinkles and "retacking" points that you tacked earlier.

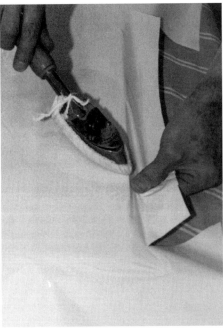

3-6. After you've tacked the film at the root and tip ribs, return to the trailing edge, and pull and tack midway between the first tack points.

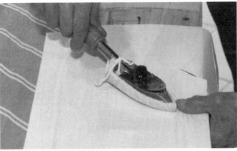

3-7. On the leading edge, pull and tack the film at places halfway between previous tack points.

3-8. Note the excess material at the wing tip.

COVERING THE WING TIP

The tips of most wings require less covering film than the chord. The wrinkles that you see in Photo 3-8 were caused by excess material. Dilemma?—not really. Covering film shrinks, so the next step will be to shrink the excess material *before* you seal the film onto the tip.

Although a heat gun will expedite the shrinking process, you can also use a hot iron. Lift the loose covering from the tip so that it won't stick to the tip or itself while you're shrinking it. (See Photo 3-9.) Also, make sure that the side with adhesive doesn't fold under and stick to itself.

Working slowly, shrink the material by applying heat as shown in Photo 3-10. (If you use a heat gun, you'll probably want to wear a glove. Heat guns can reach temperatures in excess of 400 degrees Fahrenheit.) Shrink the material until it seems as if you no longer have enough of it to cover the tip.

Now it's time to seal the film to the tip. While you apply the heat, pull the material hard toward the tip's leading edge. As shown in Photo 3-11, the film will stick as you pull it down. Follow the same procedure at the tip's trailing edge. If there's still excess material at the tip's center, shrink the film more before you proceed.

As you work toward the tip's center from both the leading and the trailing edges, it will shrink and stretch at the same time.

SHRINKING WHILE STRETCHING

You shrink the film by applying heat to the upper surface, while you stretch it by pulling it around the tip's rounded edge. (See Photo 3-12.) Continue to heat it and pull it until all the wrinkles have gone and the tip is well-defined. At that point, use your iron to seal the film down—but only at the top of the tip, where the roundness begins. (See Photo 3-13.)

To apply the covering around the tip, stretch it over the top of the edge, and then shrink it as you wrap it around the bottom. Working only $1/16$ to $1/8$ inch at a time, pull the covering around the edge. Work from the leading edge to the trailing edge and back again. Slowly stretch the covering around the tip while you heat and shrink the covering that hasn't been sealed down. You must shrink

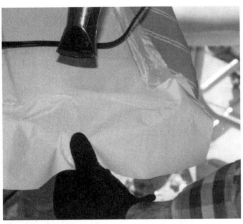

3-9. Lift the loose material off the tip while you shrink it.

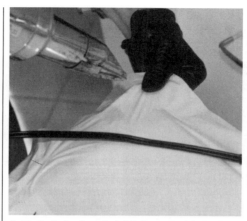
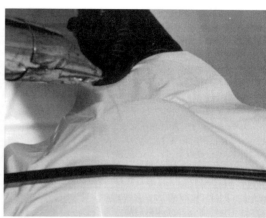

3-10. Apply heat, and shrink the material slowly. If you use a heat gun, be sure to wear a glove to protect your hand.

3-11. As you pull the heated material down over the tip, it becomes tacked into place.

the covering because, as you move around the edge, less and less material will be needed. Photo 3-14 shows the top covering being applied.

Direct the point of the iron to deliver heat to the loose covering, while you use its heel to seal the stretched material. At this point, there's a lot of tension on the covering, and when the adhesive is hot, the covering has a tendency to pull loose. Hold the sealed-down covering in place for a few seconds after you've removed the heat. (See Photo 3-15.) This will prevent any slipping, pulling, or shifting while the adhesive cools. After you've sealed the covering about 1/8 inch beyond the center line of the edge, trim it with a sharp blade as shown in Photo 3-16. Finally, iron it with a wiping motion.

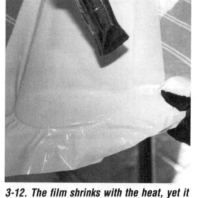

3-12. The film shrinks with the heat, yet it stretches as it's pulled down over the tip.

LEADING AND TRAILING EDGES

When you've finished the tip, seal the leading and trailing edges into place. On the trailing edge, seal and trim the material so that it's level with the upper surface. (The upper covering will later overlap the bottom covering to strengthen the seam between the two pieces.) On the leading edge, allow the material to overlap the upper surface by about 1/8 inch above the edge's center line. A metal straightedge will help you to make the trim cut. (See Photo 3-17.)

This is one of the few times that you'll use pressure with your iron to push down the covering. Gently press the edge of the material on the leading edge "into" the wood. Iron with a wiping action, and work from the covered side of the leading edge to the trimmed edge of the film. The pressure and the wiping action tend to "bevel" the cut edge so that it will later disappear under the top covering. A little adhesive may ooze onto the

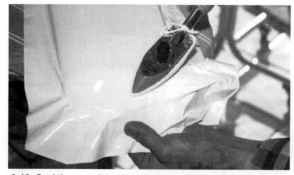

3-13. Seal the material only at the top of the tip, where the roundness begins.

3-14. Shrink the film as you apply it to the edge. (Here, the top covering is being applied.)

bare wood, but don't be troubled by this. You'll cover it later.

The top covering should overlap the leading edge's center line by at least $1/8$ inch. (See Photo 3-18.) When you apply the upper covering, allow it to overlap the bottom covering by about $1/4$ inch. This will create a tightly sealed fuelproof bond, and it will put the seam (if visible at all) on the bottom side of the wing.

One final note: you won't ever be able to wrap strip ailerons with one piece of film, so don't bother trying. Two pieces always work better.

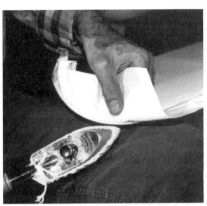

3-15. After you've removed the heat, hold the material in place for a few seconds while the adhesive cools.

3-16. Trim off the excess material with a sharp blade.

3-17. It's best to use a straightedge (not shown) to trim the leading-edge material.

STAB, FIN AND RUDDER

Treat solid wooden pieces, such as the stab, the fin and the rudder, just like the wing. Stretch the covering and tack it until it's free of wrinkles. Don't be tempted to iron the covering to the flat surface of the wood, because you'll seal it into the grain. Instead, use the heat gun to do the final shrinking—just as you did on the wing.

As shown in Photo 3-19, you should cut a slot in the stabilizer covering to allow hot air to escape from the area between the wood and the covering. This slot will be covered by the fin later. On rudders, elevators and, sometimes, fins—parts that are entirely visible after they've been installed—you won't be able to cut such a slot. Instead, leave unsealed spaces along the edge of the hinge surface. Shrink the covering over the rest of the surface until it's tight, as shown in Photo 3-20. Then, go back and pull the unsealed sections tightly over the edge while you seal them with your trim iron. (See Photo 3-21.)

In the next chapter, I discuss how to use all these techniques—and a few new ones—to cover the fuselage.

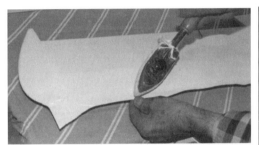

3-18. The top covering should overlap the leading edge center line by at least $1/8$ inch.

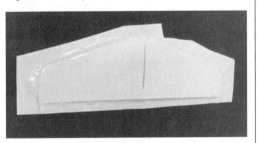

3-19. Cut slots in the covering to allow hot air to escape.

3-20. Shrink the film over the surface until it's tight, but don't seal it with an iron.

3-21. Finally, seal the unsealed sections along the edges with a trim iron.

4

Covering
Fuselages

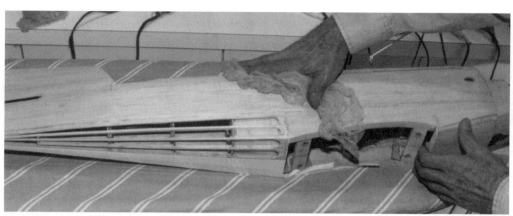

4-1. Wipe down the fuselage twice with a tack cloth.

As with wings, stabs and control surfaces, the general rule for covering fuselages is to cover from the bottom to the top. This technique will hide as many seams as can be hidden. Before you begin, remember to wipe the fuselage twice with a tack cloth as shown in Photo 4-1.

It's easiest to cover a box-type fuselage in four sections: the bottom, the two sides and, finally, the top. Whether the fuselage is made of solid wood or built-up stringers, the procedure is the same. Tack and stretch the film across the bottom, as though it were a stab or a wing. Seal it along the edges just as you would along a wing's leading and trailing edges. Use a heat gun or an iron to do the final shrinking, but don't press down with the iron. You only want to shrink the film, not seal it to the fuselage panel. Cover the sides and the top of the fuselage in the same manner.

If the fuselage is oval, you can cover it as though it had no bottom or top—just two sides.

4-2. This fuselage will be covered using two pieces of film. The seam will run along the middle of the top and the bottom of it.

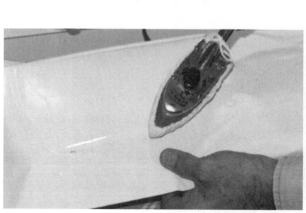

4-4. Pull the covering tight while you tack it down.

4-3. Cut an oversize piece of film—just as if you were covering a wing—and lay it over one side of the fuselage.

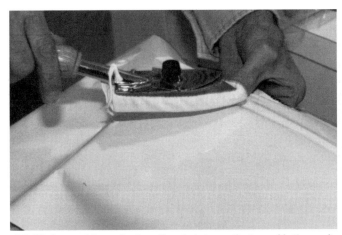

4-5. Work around the perimeter; alternate between the top and bottom and fore and aft ends, just as if you were covering a wing.

4-6. After the film has been tacked down, shrink it with a heat gun while you pull it taut.

The seam will run along the center line of the top and the bottom of the fuselage. The rounder the fuselage cross section, the better this technique will work. As with strip ailerons, you'll need two pieces of film to wrap a fuselage.

Most fuselages are shaped differently fore and aft of the cockpit. The forward section usually has a semicircular cross section, while the turtle deck has more of an oval shape.

THE TWO-PIECE COVERING TECHNIQUE

Despite its unusual shape, you can easily cover the fuselage shown in Photo 4-2 using the "two-piece" technique. Just shrink the film over the open areas in exactly the same way as you would over solid areas, and seal it to the wood only at the joints.

Cut a piece of film so that it's larger than the area you plan to cover; there should be about 2 inches of extra material all around. (See Photo 4-3.) Tack down the film while you pull it taut, and work around the perimeter. (See Photos 4-4 and 4-5.) After you've tacked the film into place, pull it taut while you shrink it with a heat gun. Remember to work slowly. (See Photos 4-6 and 4-7.)

In Photo 4-8, one side of the fuselage has been finished except for the detail around the cockpit. Notice that this includes the slot for the stab; it can be cut open and trimmed later. (You also may have

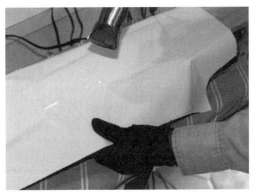

4-7. Work slowly across the entire surface.

noticed that the front section of the fuselage hasn't been covered. It will be covered later using film of a different color.)

It's impossible to create a straight seam along the center line without using a straightedge. (See Photo 4-9.) If you have a steady hand, just hold the straightedge in place while you cut the first side. If your hands are shaky, however, tape one end of the straightedge to the rear of the fuselage as shown in Photo 4-10, and hold the other end in place while you cut. Be very careful not to cut into the wood under the film.

The film on the first side should overlap the

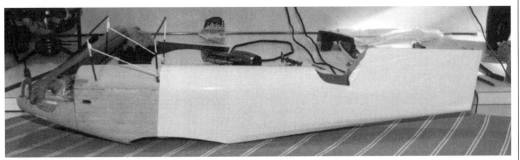

4-8. Notice that the stab slots have been covered over; they can be opened and trimmed later.

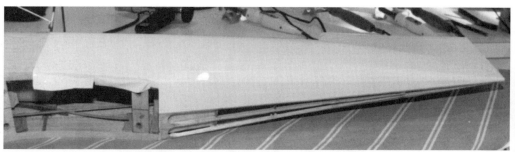

4-9. The finished side of the fuselage; the seam was trimmed using a straightedge as a guide.

4-10. Tape the straightedge into place for a more precise cut.

center line by about $^1/8$ inch. The film on the second side should also be allowed to overlap the center line by $^1/8$ inch. This will result in a $^1/4$-inch-wide seam—more than wide enough to create a tight bond. (Actually, a $^1/8$-inch-wide seam would be sufficient, but making it would be a little more difficult.)

If you trimmed the first side without cutting the wood, can you trim the second side's overlap along the seam without cutting the film beneath it? Maybe, but it's risky. Here's a solution: don't seal the second side all the way to the center line. Stop about $^1/4$ inch short of it, and tack and seal the film near—but not over—it. (See Photos 4-11 and 4-12.) Slide a thin piece of plastic under the film, and pull the film over it so that the film is taut along the center line. Now, you can safely trim the film using a straightedge as a guide. When you've finished, simply remove the plastic and excess film as shown in Photo 4-13, and seal the seam with an iron.

If you want to cover the top of the fuselage with a film of a different color than that used on the bottom, you can also use this "straightedge" trimming technique. And, by the way, using different colors is one of the best ways to hide a seam.

If the stab and the fin have been attached to the fuselage before it has been covered, try this. Before you begin to cover, seal simple "fillets," i.e., $^1/4$- or $^3/16$-inch-wide strips of film that are folded in half lengthwise, into the joints made by these pieces and the fuselage. The fillets not only seal the joints, but they also provide places for you

4-11. The covering on the second side is about to be wrapped over the center line.

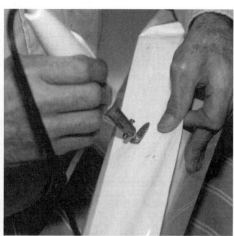

4-12. Seal and tack the film about $^1/4$ inch short of the center line. The final cut has yet to be made.

4-13. Cut the seam with the aid of a straightedge and a protective plastic sheet that's held underneath the film while it's being cut. Then just remove the plastic and peel away the excess film.

4-14. To cover compound curves—such as the curved outer edge of a stab surface—stretch the film over the high points, and then shrink it around the sides.

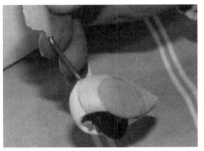

4-15. With practice, you'll be able to cover a wheel pant using just two pieces of film.

to attach the final covering without having to "press" it into the wood. (Note: they'll be completely hidden under the covering.)

COVERING COMPOUND CURVES

Although covering complex surfaces such as cowls and wheel pants takes patience, the stretch/shrink qualities of iron-on film will enable you to obtain a beautiful finish. Envision trying to completely wrap an egg in a sheet of paper that's too small, i.e., there isn't enough paper to cover the high point of the egg, but there's more than enough to cover its sides. Now envision the same situation, but replace the paper with a piece of rubber. You could stretch the rubber over the high point,

4-16. A top view of the wheel pant after one of its sides has been covered.

and it would contract around the sides. With covering film, something very similar happens. You heat the film while you pull it and stretch it over the high points, and then you shrink it around the sides—like on a wing tip. (See Photo 4-14.)

Depending on the size of the object, you can use either an iron or a heat gun. If the object is small

and you use a gun, be sure to wear a glove to protect the hand that holds the film. (Note that the built-up-balsa tail-wheel pant shown in Photos 4-15 to 4-20 was covered using an iron; for parts this small, an iron is best.)

As with the fuselage, it would be easiest to cover this wheelpant in four sections. With practice, however, you'll be able to do it using two pieces of film as shown in Photos 4-15 and 4-16. (Note that the seam runs along the center of the top and bottom.)

Working slowly from the high point toward the outer edges, stretch the film and seal it. This is one of the times when you must iron the film onto the wood. As you do so, the wheel pant will begin to take shape through the covering. Then, simply make the seam, trim the excess material, and repeat the process on the other side. The finished wheel pant will appear to have a high-gloss paint job. (See Photos 4-17 to 4-20.)

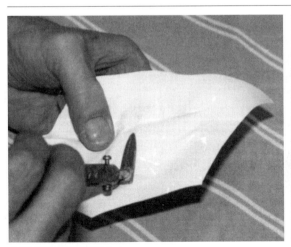

4-17. When you cover a wheel pant, iron the film directly onto the wood.

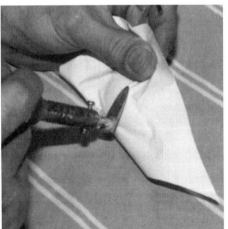

4-18. The wheel pant slowly begins to take shape underneath the covering material.

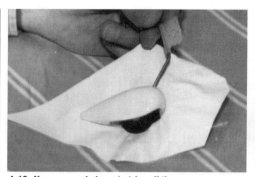

4-19. Now, you only have to trim off the excess.

4-20. The covered pant looks painted!

RECESSED AREAS

Be sure to cover recessed areas, such as air scoops in cowls, before you cover the outer surface. This will enable you to apply the outer covering in one piece and cut the material out of the recesses later. (See Photo 4-21.) Doing this in the reverse order is very difficult, and the seams in the recessed areas are almost always "raw" and visible.

When you've finished the final covering, feel around with your finger to find the recesses. With the tip of your iron, roll the covering around the edges of and into the recesses. (See Photo 4-22.) When you cut out the excess, leave about $1/16$ inch of film around the inside of each recess. Iron this film inward to create tight, almost invisible seams as shown in Photo 4-23.

4-21. Cover the interior of the recessed areas, such as those shown in this cowl, before you cover the outer surface.

You should also cover flat surfaces, e.g., the front of a cowl or the flat surface at the aft end of a fuselage, before the sides. This provides a very good surface for adhesion, and the outer covering will hide any raw edges.

In the case of a two-piece cowl, you don't need to make any seams. Use one piece for each half, and seal the covering along the flat edges of the halves where they're joined.

ENGINE-COMPARTMENT DETAILS

Speaking of cowls, all the areas where the covering overlaps into the engine compartment must be fuelproofed. Brush epoxy or sealing resin along the film's edges to ensure that fuel won't creep under them. If this happens, the fuel will not only loosen the covering, but it will also impregnate the wood, making it almost impossible to recover. This little extra precaution now will help you avoid big problems later.

Most of the stick-on trim sheets and tapes succumb to fuel sooner or later. Trimming with "heat-shrinkable" iron-on film like MonoKote guarantees a fuel-proof finish. And you'll really have fun choosing the colors you'll use. (I cover trimming and detailing with iron-on film later.)

4-22. After you've covered the interior of the recesses, cover the outer surfaces—including the recesses. Then cut some of the covering out of the recess, and seal the rest of it inward.

4-23. The finished cowl.

You can really enhance the scale appearance of your airplanes with panel lines. Unlike those made with striping tape, panel lines made with iron-on film (see Photo 5-1) won't be ruined by fuel or by being wiped down with a towel. Another big advantage of using iron-on film is the variety of colors that it comes in.

On a full-size red airplane, the panel lines look dark red, not black; on an aluminum airplane, they look dark silver; on a white or black aircraft, they look light or dark gray, and so on. For a scale appearance, make your panel lines using colors that are a variation of the background color, rather than black. (Refer to the Color Chart.) Also, be sure to switch to a film of the appropriate color whenever a panel line passes through insignias or other sections that have been covered in different colors. (See Photo 5-2.)

Panel lines are easy to make, and it's fun to show them off at the field or at a contest. There aren't any tricks; just a couple of techniques that will enable you to cut those little, skinny strips out of film accurately.

5-1. This MiG's appearance was greatly improved by the addition of panel lines. (It took third place in both Sport Monoplane and MonoKote at the '91 Toledo show.)

Panel Lines

sure to stop just short of one side to create the "tab" as shown in Photo 5-3. (This tab will be useful later.)

Lay your T-square or straightedge on the film, and position your ruler at a right angle to it as shown in Photo 5-4. Cut a $^3/_{64}$-inch-wide strip, and then continue to move the T-square/straightedge up from the bottom by $^3/_{64}$ inch after each successive cut. (Note: if you make the panel lines any thicker, your model may look like an ARF.) Cut the strips only to the tab that you created earlier; this will enable you to keep them together until you're ready to use them. Then, you can cut and apply them one at a time so you'll always know which side has the adhesive. (See Photo 5-5.)

With a metal T-square, you only have to measure one side (right side in the photos) of the film before you cut. The "T" ensures that the measurement is true on both sides of the film. Each cut will be straight unless the film is moved.

5-2. To ensure that your panel lines will be realistic, switch the lines to a film of the appropriate color whenever the color of the background changes, i.e, in insignias, etc.

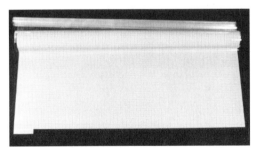

5-3. Using a straightedge or a T-square as a guide, cut the edge of the film so that it's perfectly straight and true.

TOOLS AND TECHNIQUES

For tools, you need only your trusty old modeling knife and a lot of no. 11 blades, a metal straightedge (or, better yet, a metal T-square), a ruler with $^1/_{64}$-inch increments and a flat, smooth cutting surface (glass is best).

Remove the backing from the film, and place the film on the glass. Rub it with a soft cloth (preferably cotton) to remove all the wrinkles and to make it stick. If it doesn't stick tightly, remove it and moisten the glass with glass cleaner. Then, rub it again to remove wrinkles and bubbles.

Once the film is in place, you must ensure that its lower edge is straight so that the cut lines on your first strip will be true. Using your T-square or straightedge as a guide, cut off the lower edge. Be

COLOR CHART	
Black panel lines are rarely recommended because they don't look realistic. The colors you use should depend on the background film. Here are some suggestions using MonoKote shades:	
Background Color	**Panel-Line Color**
White	Dove Gray
Black	Dove Gray, Metallic Charcoal, Platinum
Aluminum	Platinum, Metallic Charcoal
Red	Dark Red
Dark Red	Maroon, Red
Dark Blue	Medium Blue, Light Blue
Medium Blue	Dark Blue
Light Blue	Medium Blue
Yellow	Cub Yellow, Dove Gray
Orange	Cub Yellow, Tan, Yellow
Olive	Metallic Charcoal
Platinum	Metallic Charcoal, Aluminum
Metallic Charcoal	Black, Platinum
Most other metallics	Platinum

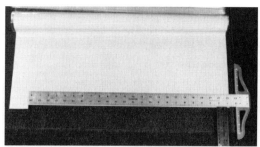

5-4. After each cut, you can move the T-square up in ³⁄₆₄-inch increments with a ruler, measuring as you go.

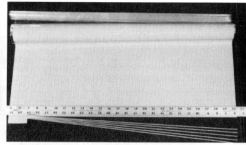

5-5. Note that the panel lines remain attached on one side of the cut.

Although it requires a little more time, you can achieve the same results using an ordinary metal straightedge. Press down on it to prevent it from moving while you measure first one side of the film and then the other. Go back and check that these measurements are accurate. You'll probably have to do this more than once, because it's easy to skew the measurement whenever you move the straightedge into position on either side. Do your best to make each strip exactly the same width so that, later, you'll be able to join two of them to create long panel lines.

ATTACHING THE PANEL LINES

Attaching panel lines to a covered model is much easier than you might think. Because iron-on film can be stretched without heat, you can stretch the strips that you made into straight lines across the surface of the model.

First, tack one end of the strip into place with a hot iron (for MonoKote, about 300⁺ degrees Fahrenheit). Then gently pull the other end until the strip is stretched flat across the surface. Hold the strip taut while you tack down the other end. (See Photo 5-6.)

Don't run the iron along the strip yet; this will stretch the film and create excess on one end, wrinkles, or a wavy line. Instead, tack the center of the strip (as shown in Photo 5-7), and then halfway between the center and each end. Continue to tack at the halfway points between previous tacks until the strip is fastened into place. Then, gently run the iron from one end to the other Let the heat do the work; don't use pressure.

Sometimes, a panel line will intersect one that you applied earlier. When this happens, you'll have to cut the "second" strip so that it overlaps and forms a "T" with the one you first applied. (Do the cutting after both lines have been tacked into place.) At the intersection, lift the second strip off the first, slide a thin piece of clear plastic under it, and cut it so that it's square with the edge of the first. (See Photo 5-8.) This technique ensures a good fit and prevents you from cutting the covering or the first panel line. It also makes it easy to cut angled intersections.

As I noted earlier, you should avoid sealing the covering to the wood, except where necessary. Don't panic if this happens when you apply the panel lines. You can correct the situation using very sticky, "high-tack" tape, e.g., packing tape or electrical tape. Press a piece of it firmly on the covering, alongside—but not on—the panel line. (See Photo 5-9.) When you pull up the tape, the covering should be pulled up with it. If you really nailed it down, however, you might have to repeat this two or three times.

Follow these steps carefully, and your colleagues at the flying field will wonder how you managed to achieve such a high-quality trim job.

5-6. Tack one end of the panel line down, stretch it across the surface, and then tack the other end.

5-7. Tack the center and then halfway between the center and each end. Tack at the midpoints between previous tacks until the strip is fastened in place. Then, run the iron down the panel line.

5-8. At intersections, a clear piece of acetate or plastic facilitates the cutting of a panel line that's square with the edge of the line that it overlaps.

5-9. If you accidentally seal the film to the wood while laying down a panel line, you can pull it up using tape; just don't pull on the panel line itself.

6

Stars

Making fancy trim schemes with stars is easy using iron-on film. You can make the stars in whichever sizes and colors you like and, more important, they'll be impervious to fuel. (See Photo 6-1.)

MAKING A TEMPLATE

You can make a star with any number of points as long as the number can be divided evenly into 360—the number of degrees in a circle. For example, a five-point star is fine because 360 degrees divided by five (points) equals 72 degrees.

On a piece of paper or cardboard, draw a circle that's the size you'd like your star to be. (It will appear to be larger than the finished star, so you may want to experiment a little.) For a five-point star, use a protractor as a guide to make a mark every 72 degrees on the circle's circumference, i.e., at 0, 72, 144, 216 and 288 degrees. (See Photo 6-2.) These are the star's five points; connect them, and then determine and mark the intersections at the base of each as shown in Photo 6-3.

To make the pattern, redraw the circle on a piece of thin acetate, and place it over the star that you drew on paper/cardboard. Mark the outer points and base intersections, and make a small hole at each. (See Photo 6-4.) The holes should only be large enough to accommodate the tip of a fine-line marker so that you'll be able to make marks on the iron-on film.

Rub the film onto a piece of glass. (If it doesn't stick firmly, moisten the glass with glass cleaner, and rub the film again to remove all wrinkles and bubbles.) Make marks on the film through each of the holes in the pattern. (See Photo 6-5.) Remove the pattern and, using a straightedge as a guide, cut

6-1. This MiG sports a star made of iron-on film.

the film from one dot to the next, i.e., from each point to its corresponding base intersections as shown in Photo 6-6.

This inexpensive, easy-to-make acetate pattern enables you to create stars with very straight edges and crisp points. (See Photo 6-7.) Whenever you make a pattern of a different size, keep it on hand for future projects.

6-2. To create a five-point star, use a protractor to make marks on a circle at 0, 72, 144, 216 and 288 degrees.

DRESSING UP YOUR STARS

Small stars look fine by themselves. Large stars, such as the one in Photo 6-8, look very plain, so you need to dress them up. The easiest way to do this is to create a border by applying strips of film along either the outside (Photo 6-9) or the inside (Photo 6-12) of the star's edges.

If you choose to frame the outside of the star, use a color that will complement both the background color and the star. In places where two

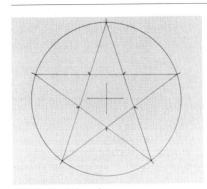

6-3. Connect the points and base intersections as shown.

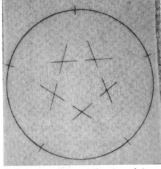

6-4. Lay acetate or other template material over the pattern, and make small holes at the outer points and the base-line intersections.

6-5. Lay the film on glass, and make marks on it through each of the holes in the pattern. (This photo shows the film after the dots have been marked.)

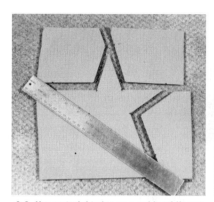

6-6. Use a straightedge as a guide while you cut the film from one dot to the next.

6-7. The result is a perfectly proportioned star.

6-8. This star needs to be dressed up a little.

6-9. Strips of film (in a color that complements both the star and the background covering) frame this star to create the border.

6-11. Slide a thin sheet of plastic under the over-lapped strips to protect the background covering while you cut them.

6-10. Apply the strips so that they overlap, and tack them into place where the ends meet.

6-12. To create a border that's the same color as the star, put thin strips of film (here, it's of a lighter color) along the inside of the star's edges.

strips meet, allow them to overlap, and tack them into place where they meet. (See Photo 6-10.) To protect the underlying base covering, slip a thin sheet of plastic under the overlapping strips. Cut both strips at the same time, as shown in Photo 6-11. Then, to create a perfect "butt fit" at the joint, press the strips with an iron.

To create a border that's the same color as the star, apply the strips of film along its inside edges. (In photo 6-12, the strips are the same color as the background covering. If you use a third color, the star will appear much smaller, but it will have a double border.) Tack the strips along the edges, leaving a gap that's as wide or as narrow as you want. (Don't be afraid to experiment. One approach—not shown here—is to make the strips and the gap the same width.) Use the cutting technique that I outlined earlier to trim the strips, and, voilà, your star has a border.

You can use this technique to create borders around just about any shape. The zigzag arrow on the airplane in Photo 6-1 was given a border using this technique, as was the tip of the fin/rudder.

To dress things up even more, experiment with combinations of stars in a variety of sizes and colors. Put little stars inside big ones or inside circles and trim lines; use the stars to form characters or numbers. With iron-on film, it's all very easy to do, and the stars won't peel off.

7

Scallops

Simple stripes can certainly add to the appearance of a model. But, if you feel like creating something really eye-catching, try making scallops. They're slightly more difficult to make than stripes, because they involve a little arithmetic. First, you must experiment on paper to determine how many scallops to make, how they should be shaped and how large they should be. To decide on their size, be sure to take the size of your model into consideration. In addition, you may want to use scallops of different sizes on the wing, the stab, the fuselage, etc.

In this chapter, I outline how to put scallops on a wing. The techniques that I describe, however, can be used to apply them to any section of your airplane.

SCALLOPS ON A WING
The wings are a good place to start. The scallops should run either from the wing tip to the side of the fuselage or from one wing tip to the other. How many scallops should you make? Well, think in terms of the number of "points" the scallops will have. As a rule, the outer points should merge with the wing tips. But, on low wings, they can also merge with the fuselage.

First, draw several small, scale planforms of the wing so that you can experiment with different numbers of scallops in a variety of shapes and sizes. Photo 7-1 shows some of my experiments. In Sketches A and B, the scallops merge with a solid band of color that runs across the chord of the center of the wing. In A and B, the bands on each wing half are half the width of the fuselage. In Sketches C and D, the scallops continue all the way to the center. When I reached Sketch D, I real-

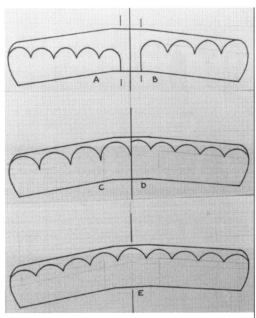

7-1. Here are some of my "scallop" experiments. I liked what I had achieved in Sketch D, so I repeated the pattern in Sketch E.

ized that a scallop "on center" would look good. So I settled on Sketch E.

Sketch E has 10 points and, therefore, nine scallops. An even number of scallops would put a point in the middle of the wing, as in Sketch C. Either one looks good; it's simply a matter of preference.

Once you've chosen a design, you can make a full-size plan. The example wing in Photo 7-2 has a 60-inch span. To figure out where to mark the

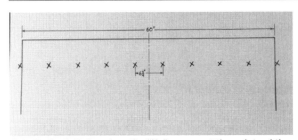

7-2. On the full-size plan, the "Xs" represent the points of the scallops.

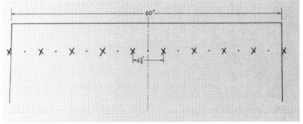

7-3. The dots halfway between the "Xs" represent the centers of the semicircles that you'll cut to create the scallops.

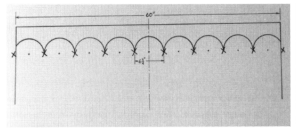

7-4. The size of these semicircles will determine how thin the sections that taper to the points will be.

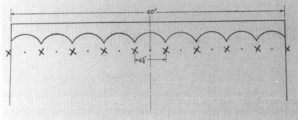

7-5. Scallops made using 8-inch-diameter semicircles over points that are $6^3/4$ inches apart. Note the short tapered sections.

7-6. Make a pattern out of poster board or stiff paper. (The hole in this pattern was made to accommodate aileron pushrods.)

You can experiment with your compass to make larger half circles, or you can follow my rule of thumb (and, no, it isn't hard). Simply increase the diameters of the semicircles by adding $3/16$ inch for every inch of diameter. This will create a nice overlap. Now, multiplying $6^3/4$ inches by $3/16$ is too complicated. Round up to 7 before you do the multiplication: 7 times $3/16$ equals $1^5/16$. Add this to $6^3/4$ inches, and you get an $8^1/16$-inch-diameter semicircle—again, too complicated. Round off to 8 inches. (No hard rules, remember?) In Photo 7-5, 8-inch-diameter semicircles have been drawn to scale.

Once you've decided on the shape and size of the scallops, make a pattern out of poster board. (See Photo 7-6.) Set your compass, draw the pattern and use scissors to cut it out. You won't use this pattern as a guide to cut the scallops out of film so that you can lay them on the background covering. Rather, you'll use it as a guide to trim the background covering to accommodate the scallops.

points on it (indicated by the "Xs"), divide 60 inches by 9 (the number of scallops), which will give you 6.666 inches. For simplicity, round this to $6^3/4$ inches. Now, 9 times $6^3/4$ inches equals $60^3/4$, which is $3/4$ inch too much. That's OK, though, because the points at the tips don't need to extend as far toward the trailing edge as the others. (Refer to Sketch E in Photo 7-2.)

After you've marked all 10 points, make marks halfway between them (indicated by the dots in Photo 7-3). These marks represent the centers of the semicircles that you'll cut to form the scallops. Notice that the marks, like the points, are $6^3/4$ inches apart. This might cause you to jump to the conclusion that the diameters of the semicircles will be $6^3/4$ inches. They could be, but scallops don't look very good when the sections that taper to the points are long and skinny as shown in Photo 7-4. In addition, these tapered sections are hard to cut, and they don't stick very well. The solution is to increase the diameter of the semicircles so that the scallop points will be *above* the center points.

7-7. To cut the scallops, you can either use a simple compass with a modeling knife in it (left) or an X-Acto compass (right). I prefer no. 11 X-Acto blades.

CUTTING THE SCALLOPS

To cut the scallops, you'll need a simple grammar-school-type compass, a modeling knife and several no. 11 blades. (They'll quickly become too dull for this task, but you'll still be able to use them to cut wood. No waste here.) Instead of using the compass to hold a pencil or a pen, you'll use it to hold the knife. An X-Acto compass will also do the trick. (See Photo 7-7.)

Glass is the best surface on which to cut iron-on film, because it allows the knife blade to move freely in any direction. It also provides a flat surface to which the film can stick. Remove the film's

7-8. Remove the backing, lay the film down on a glass surface, and rub out all the bubbles using a soft cloth.

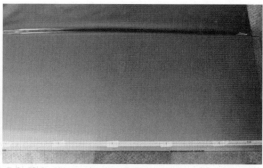

7-9. Make the marks that represent the scallops' centers on a piece of masking tape that runs along the lower edge of the film.

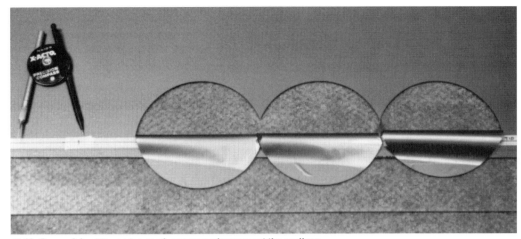

7-10. Be careful not to use too much pressure when you cut the scallops.

backing sheet, lay the film adhesive-side down, and rub it with a soft cloth to remove all the bubbles. (See Photo 7-8.)

Put a strip of masking tape along the entire length of the lower edge of the film. (If you used glass cleaner to get the film to stick, be sure the top surface is dry before you do this.) Draw a line along the tape, and make the marks that represent the centers of the scallops as shown in Photo 7-9. Put three or four layers of tape over the center marks, re-marking them each time you add a layer. The layers of tape will hold the compass point securely while you cut the scallop outlines.

Set the compass to the appropriate radius, install your knife (make sure it has a very sharp blade), and cut the semicircles. Begin and end each cut at the masking tape; the semicircles will overlap. (See Photo 7-10.) If your blade is sharp, you'll only need to press down lightly. If you use too much pressure, you might pull the film and make an irregular cut.

ATTACHING THE SCALLOPS

Make scallops for one wing half at a time. It's too hard to cut them for an entire wing—tip to tip. Leave excess material on both sides of the scallops, as shown in Photo 7-11. This will enable you to overlap the film at the center of the wing and pull it around the end of each wing tip.

If you haven't covered your wing, now is the time to do it. Apply the covering and shrink it so that it's taut. Don't spend a lot of time on the leading edge. This covering will be trimmed and removed so that the scallops have a wooden surface—not film—under them. This will minimize the possibility of bubbles.

The next step will be to remove the excess covering and replace it with the scallops. You'll put

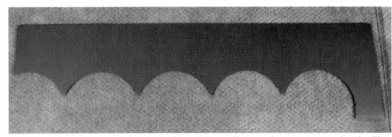

7-11. Leave excess material on both sides of the scallops so that you can overlap the film at the center of the wing and at the wing tip.

the poster-board pattern on the wing so that it's close to the leading edge. You want to ensure that the material you remove will be over the leading-edge sheeting, not over open bays. If a point does fall over a bay, you'll stop cutting $3/16$ inch ahead of the sheeting's rear edge, rather than cutting the film over the bay. In Photo 7-12, the background covering was trimmed to a point, i.e., over the sheeting, on the scallop closest to the center line,

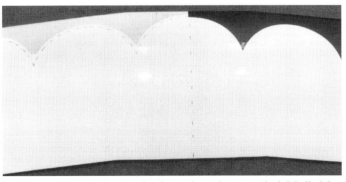

7-12. The background covering has been trimmed away on the left half of the wing, and scallops have been attached to the right half.

COVERING R/C AIRPLANES **29**

7-13. Tack the margin of film into place before you seal it down with a warm iron.

but the next scallop has a flat spot near its point, because this point is over an open bay.

Carefully tape the pattern onto the covered wing. Be especially careful with the center scallop; the wing tips are less critical. With a fine-tip mark-

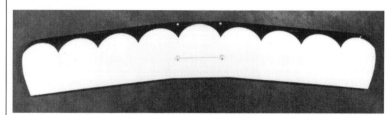

7-14. The bottom of a "scalloped" wing has been completed.

er, draw a dotted line on the film, along the outer edge of the pattern. (This line is where the scallops will fall when you put them into place.) Carefully—don't cut into the sheeting—trim away the covering, leaving a $3/16$-inch margin of film *in front of the dotted line*. (See Photo 7-12.) This excess material will form a solid fuelproof bond with the film that creates the scallops.

Remove the background covering, and seal the

margin of film to the sheeting using the tip of a hot iron. To prevent the overlap from showing through later, try to feather the edge of the film "into" the wood.

Position the scalloped material along the dotted line. Slowly and carefully tack the film into place with an iron. (For MonoKote, set the iron at about 220 degrees Fahrenheit.) Don't slide the iron along the seam, or you'll distort the scallop material. Just tack along the seam and at the leading edge and tip until everything has been aligned and all the wrinkles have been smoothed out. When the scallop material is in place, work the iron back over the points, and smooth them onto the open bay areas. (See Photo 7-13.)

Pull and stretch the material around the leading edge and seal it down, just as you would if you were covering an entire wing. To "final-seal" the seam, increase the temperature of the iron. (With MonoKote, set it at 280^+ degrees Fahrenheit.) In Photo 7-14, you can see how the finished scallops look.

If you apply scallops to both the top and bottom of the wing, allow the film to overlap itself by about $1/4$ inch. If you apply them only to the top of the wing, a straightedge should be used to trim it about $3/16$ inch beyond the center of the leading edge. This will produce a crisp "paintline" effect on the bottom of the wing.

To dress up the scallops, you can put an $1/8$-inch-wide strip of film of a contrasting color around the edges of the scallops. This technique produces a very finished, professional "pinstripe" look.

Use your imagination. You can trim the scallops in all sorts of fancy ways. Why not experiment with starbursts, teardrops, diamonds, lightning bolts, etc.? You can also combine more than one type of trim. I trimmed my biplane with scallops and flames. (See Photo 7-15.) I discuss how to

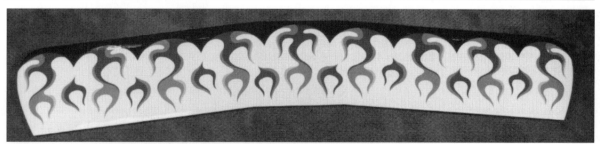

7-15. When you add flames to scallops the result is striking. Flames are discussed in the next chapter.

8

Flames

Sometimes, the more difficult something appears to be, the more driven I am to try it. I've always liked the flames that custom body shops paint on hot rods, but I know that there's a big difference between what you can do with an airbrush and what you can do with solid-color covering film. For instance, with film, you can't blend one color into another.

In one project, I decided to try for a multicolored, blended effect anyway, and I chose three colors of film that complement one another: red, orange and yellow.

Red, orange and yellow would probably look good on base colors such as metallic

8-1. A flame design for one covering project.

green, black and some of the blues, but I chose white as a base, because I had already chosen metallic plum for the scalloped trim.

In the air, the plane is purple and white with flames. Seen from just a short distance away, the red, orange and yellow blend.

DESIGNING FLAMES
The first problem was designing a flame. I pored through old car magazines. There were all sorts of flames, but I couldn't find any that would lend themselves to three colors, or that would fit well

on the wing. By combining ideas from the magazines and doing a lot of doodling, I eventually came up with the design shown in Photo 8-1.

Having penciled the flame design, including its color divisions (Photo 8-2), I realized that I'd have to make a pattern. A copy machine made this easy to do. (See Photo 8-3.) Later, I used the copier again to reduce the drawings to make flames that would fit several parts of the aircraft.

CREATING PATTERNS
For variation, I wanted to have flames moving in

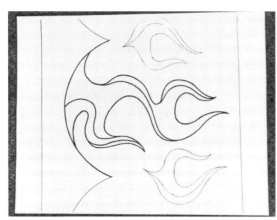

8-2. First, draw lines that show the color divisions. Use a copier to enlarge or reduce the drawing to fit various parts of the aircraft.

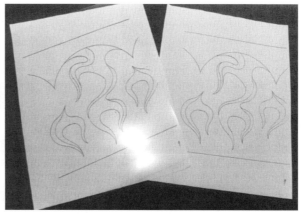

8-3. The original drawing is on the right; a copy made on clear plastic is on the left, and there's a piece of white paper underneath it.

different directions (left and right). This would usually require six patterns, one for each color going both left and right. Back to the office copier. To make patterns on clear plastic, I used the plastic film that's made for overhead projectors (sold in most stationery stores). It's only about .003 to .005 inch thick, but it's strong enough for a pattern. You can see through it and align the colors correctly while you transfer the pattern onto the MonoKote. In Photo 8-3, the original drawing is on the right, and the film copy is on the left with a sheet of white paper underneath it.

I made three sets of patterns—one for each color—and then cut out the area covered by only one color in each pattern. Simply flip the patterns over to make left and right patterns. Use the pat-

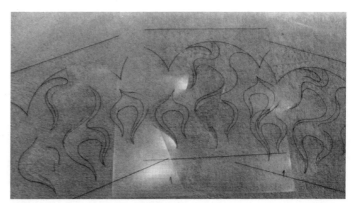

8-4. After making three copies of the pattern on clear plastic, I cut out the patterns for each color.

terns only to draw the outlines of the colors, not to guide the knife. Photo 8-4 shows the three patterns after the sections for each color had been cut out.

MARKING AND CUTTING

You must use a permanent-ink fine-tip marker to draw the pattern on the covering material. (You'll use liquid to make the two films stick together while you cut, so water-soluble markers aren't suitable.) The colors must fit perfectly together (a "butt fit" with no overlap), so the edges that will meet must be cut at the same time to ensure a good match.

To ensure a good, clean cut, cut on a flat surface. As always, glass is best; if you dampen it with glass cleaner, it will hold the first color firmly in place. (See Photo 8-5.)

After dampening the first color with glass cleaner, rub the second color over it; the glass cleaner holds the second color firmly on the first. (See Photo 8-6.) This enables you to cut through both colors with a single cut and results in their edges being perfectly matched.

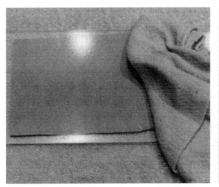

8-5. Adjacent colors must be cut at the same time. Here, one color has been smoothed onto glass.

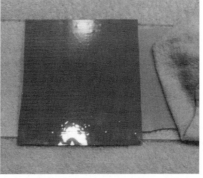

8-6. Dampen the first color with glass cleaner, and rub the second color over it. The second color will be held firmly in place. Cut both colors at once so that their edges will match.

8-7. Here, the shape of two colors that will be butted against a concave cutout have been drawn and then cut.

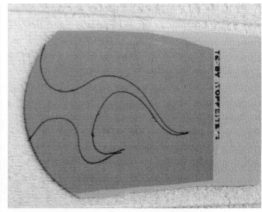

8-8. The outline of the red part of the flame—the first to be cut—has been drawn on the red plastic film, which sits on top of the orange film.

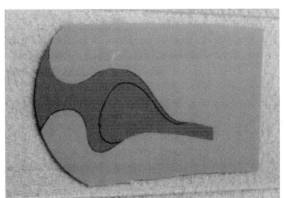

8-9. Most of the top color has been removed from the area where the bottom color will be visible in the final design.

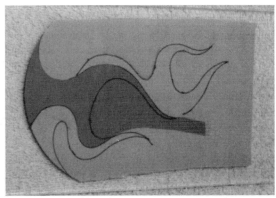

8-10. A pattern has been used to draw the outline of the first color.

Because the bottoms of these particular flames are concave, I cut the two colors at the same time to ensure a perfect fit. (See Photo 8-7.)

Using the pattern, draw the outline of the color to be cut first. Photo 8-8 shows the outline of the red part of the flame drawn on the red MonoKote, which is on top of the orange MonoKote.

Working with only two colors at a time, cut first where the colors join. *Cut the outside (outline) last* to ensure a smooth transition from one color to the next along the outside edge.

In Photo 8-9, most of the color on top has been removed from where the bottom color will be visible in the final design. Any bottom color hidden underneath other colors in the final design will be removed later—but not until the cutting has been completed and the design has been removed from the glass.

In Photo 8-10, the pattern has been used to draw the outline of the first color.

Photo 8-11 shows the two colors taped together to hold them in alignment. I've found that 3M no. 811 tape works well. It's easy to remove later, and affected very little by heat.

When all the "joining" cuts have been made and the cut areas taped for the first two colors, you're ready to start on the third color. Dampen pieces of the third color, rub them into place, and draw the outline using the pattern as shown in Photo 8-12. Then, cut the joining lines, remove the unwanted material and tape the joints.

Finally, using the patterns to align the colors, draw the final outline and make the final outside cut as noted earlier. Then take the design off the

glass, and remove any excess material that's on the underside.

ATTACHING FLAMES

The flame shown in Photo 8-13 is ready to be put

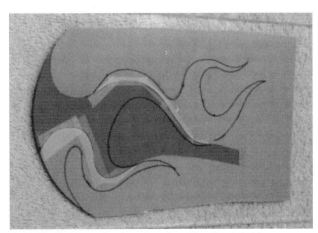

8-11. The first two colors have been taped together to hold them in alignment.

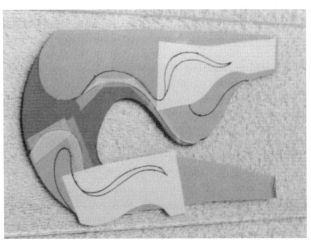

8-12. Pieces of the third color dampened and rubbed into place; the outline has been drawn using a pattern.

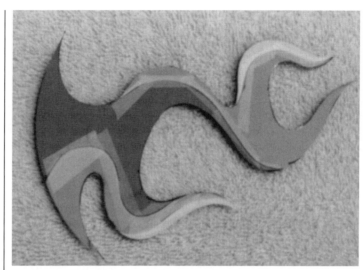

8-13. Here's a finished flame, ready to decorate a model.

8-14. To attach the flame to the covering, use a warm iron and work from the center outward. This smooths the film and pushes air out from underneath it; you don't want bubbles.

into place on the wing. The bottom of the flame can simply blend into the color of the fuselage, or it can have a shape of its own. (The convex bottom of the one shown in the Photo 8-13 has been cut to fit into a concave scallop.)

Using a warm iron (for MonoKote, 200 to 220 degrees Fahrenheit), attach the flame to the base covering. Having positioned it, work from the center outward to its edges, as shown in Photo 8-14. This technique smooths the film and pushes out any trapped air, so "bubbles" are minimal.

This process might seem tedious, but each flame takes less time to prepare than the preceding one. My first one took about an hour, but before long, I was whipping them out in about 10 minutes. The same goes for attaching them to the covering.

Photo 8-15 shows the finished design. There have to be hundreds of others that you can make with film in several colors. Just think of things like feathers, snake scales, lightning bolts, sunbursts, comet tails, etc. You're only limited by your imagination and the number of colors you have.

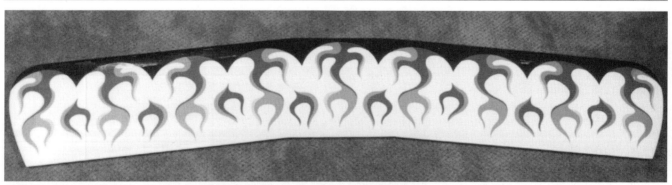

8-15. Here's a completed wing. As you gain proficiency, the flames take less and less time to make.

Rivets and other Neat Stuff

9-1. The aluminum finish on the Unitaar has been enhanced by the addition of panel lines and rivets.

After I had finished covering my first airplane with aluminum-colored film, I realized how dull aluminum looks without trim. The film was supposed to look as if it had a metal finish, but without rivets and panel lines, etc., it just looked sort of gray.

At first, drawing panel lines, rivets, access doors, etc., seemed like the easy solution. The questions of what to draw with, how to space and draw rivets and how to seal all this against fuel were enough to make me seek out a better way.

As you see in Photos 9-1 and 9-2, nicely spaced rivets and panel lines are possible. The answer to the fuelproofing problem is simple: cover the graphics with a clear covering film. When sealed down, it provides permanent, fuelproof protection and is virtually invisible.

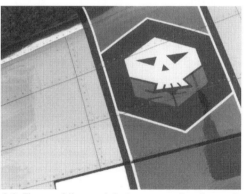

9-2. The panel lines and rivets are press-transfer graphics. Covered with clear film, they're completely fuelproof.

9-3. Letraset offers many graphics; I use 1-point lines for panel lines. They come on sheets and are available in many widths.

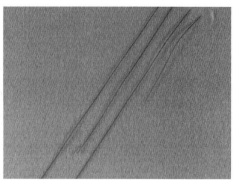

9-4. These lines have been applied to the adhesive side of clear film that has then been cut into strips. They're now ready to be ironed onto the model.

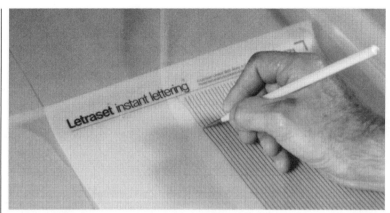

9-5. By rubbing the graphics onto the film instead of applying them directly to a finished model, you'll avoid denting the model's surface. A fair amount of pressure is required to transfer the image.

material with a stylus or an ordinary ball-point pen. By rubbing the graphics onto the clear film instead of onto the covered aircraft, you'll avoid damaging the aircraft's surface. You must rub fairly hard to transfer the image. (See Photo 9-5.)

For the "rivets," I use Chartpak RDC 1, which comes in a roll, like tape. The little circles (rivets) are equally spaced and in a straight line. This solves the spacing and alignment problem. (See Photo 9-6.)

Some panel lines look better with a row of rivets running alongside. This is easy to do, too. Just put a line and a row of rivets together on the adhesive side of the film, and cut the film into strips.

PRESS-TRANSFER GRAPHICS

As for the panel lines, rivets and other graphics, the "press-transfer" materials found in art-supply stores work perfectly. The lines come in sheet form in various widths. I used 1-point line rules, made by Letraset. (See Photo 9-3.)

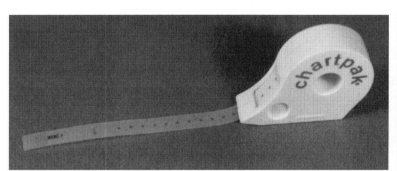

9-6. Applying straight lines of evenly spaced rivets is a breeze if you use Chartpak RDC 1, which comes in a roll.

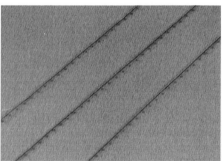

9-7. Making a panel line with a row of rivets alongside is also easy. Apply both details to the adhesive side of clear film, cut the film into strips and stick the strips onto the model.

By rubbing the lines onto the adhesive side of the clear film and then cutting the film into strips, you can make all the straight panel lines you need. (See Photo 9-4.) Rub the image onto the covering

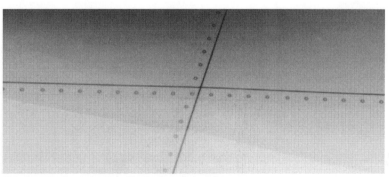

9-8. Once in place, the clear film is virtually invisible.

(See Photo 9-7.) On the airplane, the clear film is almost invisible; you see what looks like a panel secured with rivets. (Photo 9-8.) Two rows of rivets might also be appropriate; apply them in the same way.

OTHER SHAPES

If you search through the "symbol" catalogues that are provided by the makers of the press-transfer materials, you'll find a wide variety of shapes. I found some hexagonal symbols (see Photo 9-9), which are perfect for

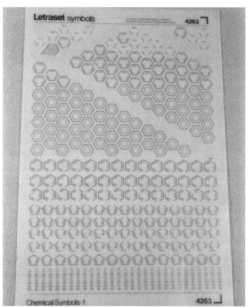

9-9. The many available symbols can be used in the same way as the panel lines and rivets.

TEST THE GRAPHICS FIRST

At first, I thought that the graphics might melt under the film when I applied heat. To my surprise, I had no problem, but it's probably worth testing them on scrap. Many manufacturers make press-transfer materials, and I'm only familiar with those I mention.

If the base covering sticks to the underlying wood as you put on the trim, you can pull it back off. Just put a "high-tack"

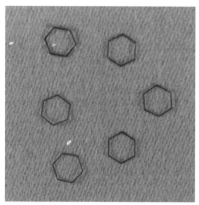

9-10. Applied to the adhesive side of clear film and cut out, these markings are ready to be applied.

tape, like packing tape, alongside the trim strip, and pull the base covering off the wood, by pulling on the packing tape. Sometimes, it will take more than one attempt to loosen the covering.

Press-transfer graphics provide unlimited possibilities for creating an aircraft that looks unique.

certain details. They were rubbed onto the adhesive side of the film and then cut out. (See Photo 9-10.) I used a "hexagon" theme throughout my Unitaar design. The airplane fuselage is hexagonal, as is the insignia on the wing. (See Photo 9-11.) Photo 9-12 shows hexagonal symbols simulating access doors near the wing tips. Hexagons with bars inside them simulate the step plates near the cockpit. (See Photo 9-13.)

You'll find circles, diamonds, stars, squares, ellipses and myriad other shapes in a variety of sizes. Some shapes come in colors. Even reverse lettering is available.

9-11. The fuselage cross section is hexagonal, so hexagonal symbols seemed in order.

9-12. Hexagonal access panels along the wing tip add detail to an otherwise plain finish.

9-13. These hexagons with bars make very convincing step plates along the side of the cockpit.

10

Multi-colored Trim Schemes

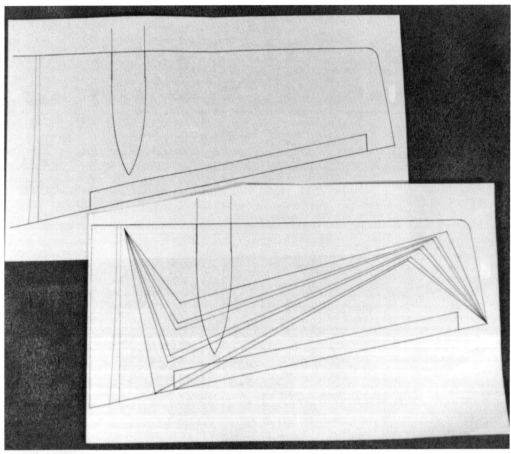

10-1. Use a copy machine to scale down the plan so that it fits on legal-size paper. Then, sketch potential designs on the scaled-down versions.

Multicolored trim schemes look great and, because iron-on film comes in so many colors, you can be very creative. It's difficult, however, to put large trim pieces over background film without getting bubbles. The answer is to trim the background film, join pieces of trim film, and tack them into place on the bare wood so that they overlap the background film.

There are two "seaming" techniques that make this easy and guarantee a fuelproof finish. Narrow overlap seams stick together well, and they prevent the underlying film from showing through. Butt seams come in handy when you make elaborate multicolored graphics, but they need to be sealed with trim strips.

In this chapter, I discuss how to put together a

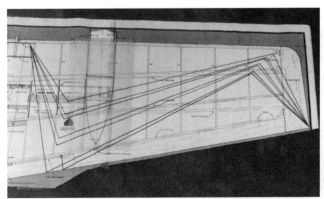

10-2. Once you've chosen a design, draw a full-size version of it on the plans.

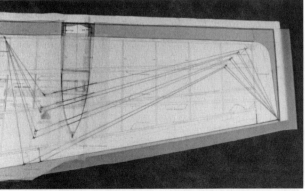

10-3. Tape a sheet of Mylar to the plans, and draw the reference marks and color intersections on it.

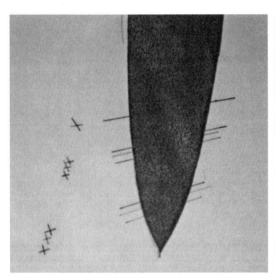

10-4. In each group of cross hairs, the center one marks the butt seam.

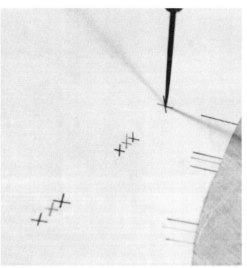

10-5. Use an awl to punch marker holes in the Mylar.

five-color scheme using both overlap and butt-seam techniques.

WORKING OUT THE DESIGN

It's easiest to work out your design on small, scale planform drawings that you've made using a copy machine. This way, you can make as many trial sketches as you like without ruining the plans. Photo 10-1 shows the planform of a Duellist wing that has been scaled down to fit on legal-size paper. The wing is the best place to create a multicolored trim design, because it's usually the largest area.

After you've decided on a design, draw a full-size version of it on the building plan, as shown in Photo 10-2. Next, make a template out of Mylar. This thin (.003- or .005-inch thick), flexible, translucent material is easy to draw on, and it holds its shape quite well. It's sold in art-supply stores in 24x36-inch and 17x22-inch sheets. Tape a sheet of it over the plan, and mark the points where the col-

ors intersect with little "cross hairs." You should also make reference marks at key ribs, spars, tip blocks, etc., so that you'll be able to remove and replace the template in exactly the same spot later. (See Photo 10-3.) When you've finished making the template, remove it from the plan.

On the design for the Duellist wing, the center cross hair in each group of three is for the butt seam, and the outer ones mark the border of the trim that will cover the butt seam. (See Photo 10-4.)

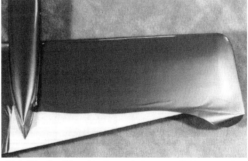

10-6. The Duellist wing has only been partially covered because its leading and trailing edges will be done in different colors.

Use an awl to punch a hole in the template at each intersection. Then, turn the template over, and trim off the excess material that was pushed through. You want the top and the bottom of the template to be smooth because you'll use it to layout the design on both wing halves.

BACKGROUND COLORS

Because its trailing edge and leading edge will each be done in a different "background" color,

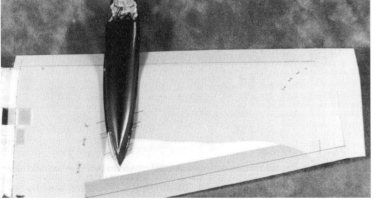

10-7. With the template on the wing, a fine-line marker was used to make dots through the holes in the template.

10-8. *Trim the background covering to accept the graphic. This covering should extend ³⁄₁₆ inch under the trim to create a good seal.*

10-9. *The second color has been added to the trailing edge and trimmed so that it extends under the graphic like the first piece. This leaves a balsa surface on which to iron the graphic.*

the Duellist wing in Photo 10-6 has only been partially covered. If the design called for one background color, you would cover the entire wing at this point.

10-10. *Choose a base color for the graphic, cut a piece of the second color, and rub it onto the base color. Use the template to help you mark the dots for the first two colors.*

To prepare the first background color for the graphic, put the template over the film on the wing, and use a fine-tip marker to make dots through the holes in the cross hairs. Don't draw lines connecting the dots; you'll cut the film using a straightedge as a guide. If you do draw lines, you'll have to wash a lot of ink off the covering, and the ink may seep through the cuts and onto the balsa while you do this.

Trim the covering to accommodate the graphic, but don't cut from dot to dot. Put the straightedge about ³/16 inch inside the dots, i.e., where the graphic will be positioned. By allowing the background film to extend under the graphics, you'll create a tight seal. (The Duellist wing is at this stage in Photo 10-8.)

Always use a new blade, and change it as soon as it begins to drag. Be careful not to cut into the wood, though. When you've finished cutting the film, iron down the freshly cut edges.

In Photo 10-9, the second background color has been added to the trailing edge and trimmed to accept the graphic in the same way as the first. This leaves a nice, clean balsa surface on which to apply the graphic.

CUTTING THE GRAPHIC
First choose a base color for the graphic. (On the Duellist wing, I made the center color the base color.) Cut the film to the approximate size, leaving extra for your reference marks. Then, remove its backing, and rub the film onto a piece of glass

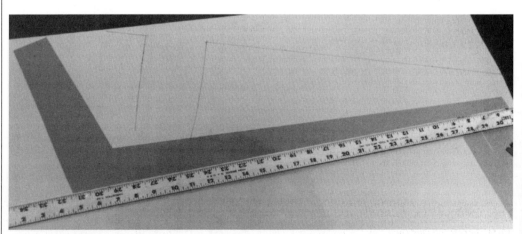

10-11. *Align a straightedge with the dots, and cut through both layers of film.*

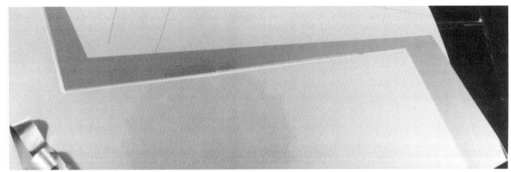

10-12. After you've completed the butt seam, remove the scrap and temporarily tape the seam with low-tack 3M no. 811 tape.

to remove any bubbles. Put the template over the film, and mark the reference lines.

Cut a piece of film of the second color, and rub it onto the base color. It should stick firmly; if not, moisten the area between the pieces of film. Rub away any bubbles, and use the template to mark the dots for the first two colors. (See Photo 10-10.) Insert a new blade in your knife and, using a straightedge as a guide, cut through both layers of film. This time, you'll connect the dots. First, cut the lines where the colors meet. These will be the butt seams, so they must be very neat. (See Photo 10-11.)

After you've cut the butt seams, remove the scrap, and tape the seams together with plastic tape as shown in Photo 10-12. (I use "low-tack," easy-to-remove 3M no. 811 tape.) Next, cut the outside edge of the graphic. (See Photo 10-13.) If you cut through the bottom layer of film, don't worry; you'll remove it later. In fact, it's good to cut through both layers just to be sure that you've cut through the top layer cleanly.

If this were a two-color graphic, you would remove the graphic from the glass, and remove the base color from underneath the second color. But, in this case, there are three colors, so everything stays in place until the third color has been added. As shown in Photo 10-14, you add the third color,

and rub it into place in the same way as you did the second color. Trim it at the butt seam, tape it to the base color (Photo 10-15), and trim its outside edge. Peel the graphic from the glass, and remove the base color from the back sides. (See Photo 10-16.)

10-13. Here, with the seam firmly taped, the outside edge of the graphic has been cut.

As you can see, the template is extremely important when you make multicolored trim schemes. Those little dots make everything come together. They're used for each color so that everything will fit perfectly, even on compound surfaces.

APPLYING THE GRAPHIC

Now, you're ready to put the graphic in place on the vacant balsa space on the wing. The dots you used to trim the background col-

10-14. Smooth the third color over the base color.

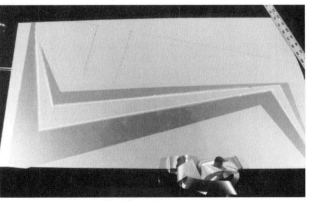

10-15. Trim the third color at the butt seam, and tape it to the base color.

ors on the wing should still be there. If they're smudged, re-mark them using the template as a guide.

Align the graphic with the dots, and gently iron it into place. Use low heat (for MonoKote, about 200 to 220 degrees Fahrenheit) to smooth it down. During this process, the tape that holds the butt seams together may buckle a little. Simply remove it as you go. This will prevent the covering from wrinkling.

Photo 10-17 shows the five-color wing, but the butt seams aren't fuelproof. In addition, the original design calls for the colors in the graphic to be separated by another color so that they appear to

10-16. After you've removed the graphic from the glass, remove the scrap film.

places as shown in Photo 10-18.

I repeated this graphic—with slight modifications—on the fuse, the stab and the rudder. (See

10-17. The butt seams on the five-color wing design still need to be sealed. If you use the background color, it will create an illusion that the graphics have been painted on the surface.

10-18. Here, the background-color trim strips have been added between the colors. They complete the graphic and fuelproof the butt seams.

be on the surface of the background color. To complete the graphic, you must cut strips of film from the background color using the template and apply them in the appropriate

Photo 10-19.) This is a fairly simple, straight-line design. But, using this technique (and your imagination) you can make many designs—including fancy curves. Remember, the template is the key.

10-19. I used slightly modified versions of this graphic on the Duellist's fuselage and its tail feathers.

O ne of the nice things about iron-on film is that it requires very little maintenance. It's important, however, to clean fuel off the film regularly—preferably after each flight, although once after every two or three flights on a given day will do. Fuel that's left on film tends to soften any raw edges along seams. This is a slow process, so if you clean the surface frequently, you probably won't have any problems.

Most window cleaners and kitchen cleaners (owing to their grease-cutting ingredients) work well. Never use a cleaner that contains an abrasive, because it will scratch the film. It's also best not to use paper towels. No matter how soft the paper might feel, it's abrasive. Use a soft cotton cloth instead. Old, worn terry-cloth towels—cut into rags—are excellent. The more you wash them, the softer they become.

Plastic cleaners are also available, but most have a little wax in them. The wax hides minute scratches, but it can also prevent the film from being sealed properly when you try to re-seal (with heat) loose seams and edges. Before you try to re-seal these areas, clean them thoroughly with alcohol to remove wax and fuel. (Note that alcohol won't affect the adhesive on most iron-on films.)

There's also an effective way to re-seal loose sections of film without using heat. Just reactivate the adhesive using a little acetone. This technique works well for the points of stars and arrows, etc., which loosen easily.

REPAIRS

It's easy to repair a puncture or a small tear: simply make an iron-on film "Band-Aid," and iron it into place. Small circles or ovals work best. In graphics such as stars, corners and points can't be avoided, but you should avoid creating them when you make patches. These areas often loosen when you rub your plane to clean it.

Before ironing on the patch, clean the surface you plan to repair. Alcohol works well for this, but it leaves a slight film. Acetone works best, but only use it if the film's coloring is on its adhesive side.

11-1. Most window/kitchen and plastic cleaners will remove exhaust residue and oil from iron-on film. Never use a cleaner that contains an abrasive.

You can make field repairs to small rips using the stick-on trim sheets that are offered by many manufacturers. You can also make temporary patches out of regular plastic tape. (Note that the adhesive on tape is compromised by fuel.)

To repair open bays on wings and fuselages, you must remove the film from the damaged section and the area that surrounds it. The object is to create a solid surface on all sides of the patch. (See Photo 11-3.) For instance, if a built-up wing had been damaged, you would remove a section of film from rib to rib and spar to spar or from the spar to the trailing edge.

Remove the film carefully. (If this section of film hasn't been damaged too badly, you can use it as a pattern to make the patch.) Thoroughly clean the surrounding surface, and re-seal the edges of the covering that remains. (See Photo 11-4.) To ensure that the patch will be sealed to the covering, make it $1/4$-inch larger—all the way around—than the area you plan to cover. (See Photo 11-5.) Tack the patch into place, seal

Maintenance and Repair

11-2. Use a soft cotton cloth to clean the film. If you want to preserve a high-quality finish, never use paper towels!

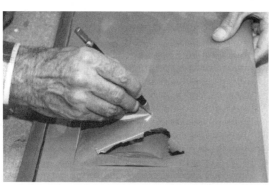

11-3. For large tears, e.g., those on a built-up wing, it's best to cut out a section of film around the damaged area to create a solid surface on all sides of the patch.

11-4. Seal the edges of the film that remains to the underlying structure.

11-5. Make the patch about ¼ inch larger—all the way around—than the area you're covering. (A contrasting color was used here for illustration.)

its edges (Photo 11-6), and heat any slack out of the center. An iron should do the trick, but for really large patches, a heat gun works best. Be sure to direct the airflow from the center of

heat to apply the covering or in places where you didn't apply the covering evenly.

To remove wrinkles, re-shrink the film using either an iron or a heat gun. A heat gun is best because you won't put pressure on the film, which would cause it to stick to the underlying surface. If the wrinkles are near seams, be sure to shield the seam from the hot air. If they're under a graphic, use an iron to remove them; a heat gun will surely loosen the graphic.

Sometimes, wrinkles will appear if you leave your airplane in a very cold or a very hot environment. Before you try to "shrink" them out, let your plane sit at room temperature (70 to 75 degrees Fahrenheit) for a day or two. Chances are that the wrinkles will disappear by themselves.

Speaking of heat, leaving an airplane in the sun all day, i.e., outside your car at the field, doesn't seem to have an adverse effect on the covering. In

11-6. Tack the patch in place so that it's smooth, and then seal the edges.

11-7. A heat gun will efficiently take any slack out of the center of a large patch. Use a piece of cardboard to protect the edges from the hot air.

the patch toward its edges. This will help to prevent the hot air from getting under the edges and loosening the seal. Better yet, shield the edges with a piece of cardboard, as shown in Photo 11-7.

What happens if you need to make a patch and you don't have any covering of the same color? Why not make the patch in a contrasting color and work it into your design? (See Photo 11-8.) No one will be able to tell that it's a patch rather than a clever color scheme.

DEALING WITH WRINKLES

On occasion, coverings that looked great when you first finished them develop wrinkles later. Most often, this occurs in places where you used excessive

fact, it seems to have a smoothing effect. If, however, you've used dark colors (which readily absorb heat from the sun) to cover your plane, all that hot sun may affect the radio equipment and Nyrods.

If you follow the guidelines noted in this chapter, your film-covered model should maintain its beautiful finish indefinitely.

11-8. This Sig Kadet Jr. wears a MonoKote disguise to simulate a Cessna. To repair a tear in one wing, I made a diagonal stripe using film that complemented the background color. For symmetry, I put a stripe on the other wing. Who would ever know that I did this because I needed to make a patch?!

The Finishing Touches

A beautifully covered airplane looks unfinished without a pilot and a decorated cockpit. Such finishing touches complement a good covering job, yet some modelers finish their aircraft simply by gluing a clear Plexiglas canopy over a flat spot on the fuse. That empty canopy turns a beautiful creation into something that reminds me of an apple with a bite taken out of it.

Some modelers go a step further by painting the inside of the canopy so that the hole won't be obvious. That's just a short cut. The same covering materials and techniques used on the outside of the aircraft should be used on the inside. A nicely finished cockpit in colors that match or complement the exterior looks so good that it's well worth the extra work.

I like to use colors in the cockpit that complement the exterior, but this is a matter of personal taste. Dove Gray goes well with light-color exteriors. I also like to create a "metallic look," e.g., use aluminum film for the side walls and the seat back, platinum film for the headrest and the area behind the seat, and metallic charcoal film for the instrument panel.

COVER THE INTERIOR

It's much easier and less time consuming to cover an interior than it is to paint it. The floor is the only section that will look better if it's painted; flat black paint seems to make it disappear.

You can easily make interior parts out of balsa or plywood. If you cover each part before you install it, you'll find it easy to devise nice color

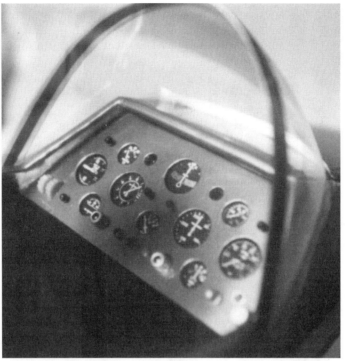

12-1. To make an instrument panel like this, drill holes for the instruments and cover the front of the panel with film. Then, mount a plastic sheet on the back of it, and glue the instrument faces to the plastic.

schemes. For instance, you can do the seat frame in one color and the seat cushion in another; you can make the trim around the instrument panel the same color as the exterior and make the panel itself darker or lighter.

When you design the cockpit details, be sure that they're appropriate for the age and style of your aircraft. For example, if you make an instrument panel, remember that older aircraft have very few instruments and military aircraft have many, etc. For spacecraft, use your imagination.

INSTRUMENT PANELS

Instrument panels can really highlight a cockpit, and $1/16$-inch-thick balsa or plywood is perfect for

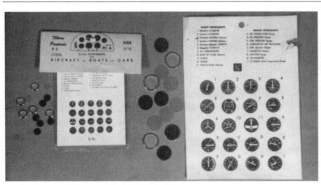 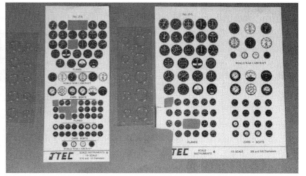

12-2 and 12-3. Here are examples of the instrument "kits" that are available. Some have molded-plastic bezels.

12-4. You don't need to use bezels to make realistic panels. This one was made for a plane that's reminiscent of a 1930s racer.

There are several instrument "kits" available. Some have metal bezels with plastic inserts; others have molded-plastic bezels. The instrument faces are printed on glossy paper and are fairly well-detailed. They come in several sizes. The building and covering techniques are the same, except holes are cut to accommodate the bezels rather than the instrument faces. The clear plastic and the black marks around the inside of the holes aren't necessary. (See Photos 12-2 and 12-3.)

Although the bezels look very nice, they aren't necessary. The curved panel in Photo 12-4 was made without them, and it was installed in an airplane designed to be reminiscent of a '30s racer. It has only a few instruments, and it's covered in Dove Gray MonoKote.

making them. Cut holes in your panel to accommodate the instrument faces you plan to use. Cover the front of it, and iron the film as far into the holes as possible before you cut it out. To give the faces depth and hide any raw edges, color the insides of the holes using a black permanent marker.

Glue a thin plastic sheet to the back of the panel to simulate the glass faces on the instruments. Position and glue the instrument faces to the plastic. (The panel in Photo 12-1 was made using these techniques and was covered in Platinum MonoKote.)

12-5. You can use pins with round heads to simulate small instrument-panel knobs.

MAKING YOUR OWN INSTRUMENT FACES

Full-scale aviation magazines frequently print pictures of instruments and instrument panels, and you can enlarge or reduce them on a copy machine to fit a model of any size. Most full-size instruments have yellow caution marks or red lines such as those on a tachometer, so you might want to color your instruments with colored pencils.

Full-scale instrument panels have a lot of knobs of various sizes. If you want to simulate them, don't use the flat heads of ordinary straight pins; they just don't look good. Instrument panel knobs are rarely ball shaped, but for the small knobs, round-head pins look OK. They're available in

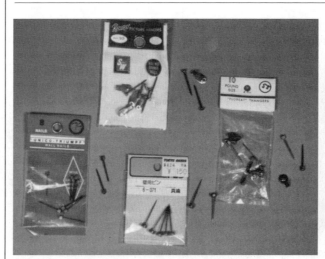

12-6. Picture-hanger nails make large, good-looking knobs.

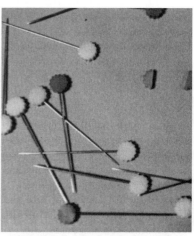

12-7. When cut in half, the heads on these pins make good switches and trim dials.

12-8. Odd instrument panels can complement unusual aircraft designs; note the laser-cannon aiming devices.

12-9. This plane features digital instruments that are backlit by a solar panel that's just in front of the cockpit. (Light is channeled to the instruments.)

sewing stores (Photo 12-5), and they're frequently used to package shirts; you probably threw some away the last time you bought a new shirt.

For large knobs, I use picture-hanger nails. They look quite realistic, and most hardware stores carry them in a variety of sizes and shapes. (See Photo 12-6.)

If you keep an eye out, you can find unusual things with which to dress up your instrument panels. While staying in a hotel once, I got a sewing kit that had pins with odd-shaped heads. When I cut them in half and glued them to the panel, they looked like aircraft switches or trim dials. (See Photo 12-7.)

I've built some weird-looking airplanes, so I've had to come up with some unusual instrument panels. The one in Photo 12-8, which is covered in black, is supposed to look like a radar screen with laser-cannon aiming devices. I gave the panel on another spacy-looking airplane radar and digital instruments that are backlit by a solar panel that's just in front of the cockpit. (See Photo 12-9.) The instrument panel is covered with aluminum MonoKote.

It's a lot of fun "inventing" a cockpit. I keep a special box for cockpit "details." Anything that even looks as if it could be made into something goes into it for future use. (See Photo 12-10.)

12-10. Don't shy away from "inventing" a cockpit using odds and ends that you've accumulated!

PILOTS

I've never tried to cover pilots with iron-on covering, and although this book is about award-winning covering techniques, it's also about win-

12-11. This headrest for high-G maneuvers was made out of a small plastic cap.

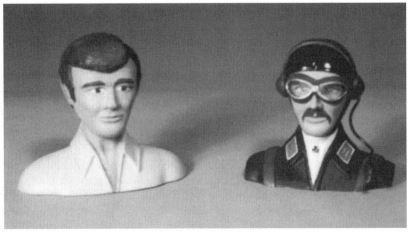

12-12. These pilots are fairly conservative, but they improved the looks of the planes they once flew.

12-13. This oddity flies the Unitaar—an airplane that resembles an X-wing spaceship.

12-14. This pilot—and the plane he flies!—can best be described as "spacy."

ning awards. I would be remiss if I didn't mention one of the most important final touches—the pilot.

Like the instrument panel, the pilot should complement the airplane. For instance, the pilot in a

12-15. This Williams Brothers pilot is made of two pieces that were glued together and then painted.

civilian aircraft shouldn't have a helmet, whereas one in a military aircraft should. The examples in Photos 12-11 to 12-16 illustrate the kinds of pilot and cockpit details that I've used in my projects. I hope they inspire you.

The headrest in Photo 12-11 was made out of a small plastic cap. (It offers the pilot support during high-G acceleration.) To make the louvers behind the seat, I used ladders from a model ship, and I used a thumb screw to make the dome-shaped device. The interior is covered with Platinum MonoKote, and the exterior is covered with Pearl Red. The stripes on the pilot's helmet are also made of MonoKote, and they match the stripes on the fuselage. To make them, I used acetone to activate the adhesive on Pearl MonoKote film, and then I put the film on a white Top Flite trim sheet. Then, I simply cut out the stripes and applied them

to the helmet. This technique works well on wheel pants and other plastic parts that can't withstand much heat.

In Photo 12-12, two fairly conventional pilots are shown. The fellow on the right used to fly a WW II Messerschmitt. (The plane was shot down, but he survived.) The fellow on the left flew a Cessna that didn't finish a fun fly.

I thought it would be appropriate to have strange characters pilot my weird-looking airplanes. The creature in Photo 12-13 flies the Unitaar, which looks like an X-wing spaceship. I put the spacy-looking guy in Photo 12-14 in another of my weird creations.

Pilots don't need to be complicated or fancy. Many companies, e.g., Williams Brothers, offer a variety of inexpensive pilot busts. To assemble them, you just glue two plastic pieces together and paint them to suit your tastes. The fellow in Photo 12-15 flies a WW II MiG for a stunt team.

12-16. Simple modifications can add realism. This pilot's head was repositioned so that he looks downward and to the left.

MAKING YOUR PILOT MORE REALISTIC

Simple modifications can make your pilot look a little more realistic. To make the pilot in Photo 12-16 look more human, I repositioned his head so that he appears to look slightly downward and to the left. Real pilots rarely stare straight ahead.

There are several things you can do to make your pilot look less like a bug-eyed statue. If you look in a mirror, you'll see that you don't have big round eyes—most people don't. If you give your pilot such eyes, he'll look like some sort of insect. In addition, don't use glossy paint on anything except the pilot's eyes or things that are naturally shiny, e.g., seat-belt buckles. A pilot with high-gloss black hair looks like a rock-and-roll star from the '50s. Use flat paint for hair, skin and clothing. You may not find it at your favorite R/C shop, so check hobby shops that sell plastic kits, doll houses, trains, etc. It comes in small bottles, and it's inexpensive. (See Photo 12-17.) It isn't fuelproof, though, so if you have an open cockpit, be sure to put a clear coat of flat fuelproof paint on your creation.

While you're at the plastic-kit hobby store, be sure to look at the decal sheets being sold. Many will make perfect emblems for a pilot's clothing and helmet. I used such decals for the shirt patch, the shoulder insignias and the helmet markings on the MiG pilot in Photo 12-15.

If you don't like the "Superman-like" features of molded-plastic pilot busts, there's an easy way to change them. I use Sig Epoxolite. It's a two-part putty that's easy to fashion into just about any shape. It sticks to plastic well, and you can paint it. I use it to make sideburns, beards, etc.

You can also find pilots in toy stores. Many dolls, both female and male, can be made into great-looking pilots, and they're usually available

12-17. Use flat paint for hair, skin and clothing. This type of paint isn't fuelproof so, if the cockpit is open, cover the pilot with a coat of clear, flat fuelproof paint.

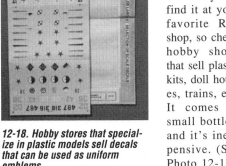

12-18. Hobby stores that specialize in plastic models sell decals that can be used as uniform emblems.

in several "scales." (See Photo 12-20.) They aren't always dressed appropriately, but that's easy to change. Don't worry if your aircraft doesn't have space for a full-figure pilot—it's nothing that a little surgery can't fix.

Finishing the cockpit and adding a pilot is really the frosting on the cake. It won't make your airplane fly any better, but you'll have fun doing it. In addition, your friends will admire it and, if you enter a contest, the judges will, too.

12-19. Sig Epoxolite is a two-part putty that you can use to change your pilot's features.

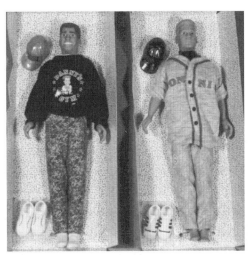

12-20. There are many dolls—male and female—that you can make into great-looking pilots.

13

Winners and Losers

13-1. The author's Twin-Twin took third place in MonoKote and second place in Sport Monoplane at the '92 Toledo show.

W hether or not you plan to enter a building contest, your work will be judged. As soon as your creation appears anywhere, the judging will start. Not everyone will say something (you know the old saying, "If you can't say something nice..."), but you'll see them squint as they look for wrinkles, bubbles and seams. It's only human nature to compare other people's work with your own.

If the comment is, "nice-looking plane," the person figures he can do better. But when it's, "How the h - - - did you get that stuff around the wing tips?," he admires your work.

To achieve a great—as opposed to just a good—covering job, there are two key areas to which you must pay particular attention: "high points" and "eye points."

HIGH POINTS
High points are surfaces that will reflect light, e.g., the tip of the vertical fin; the wing tips and leading edge; the fin/rudder tips and edges; the stab tips and leading

13-2. The compound curves of the Twin-Twin's wing tip are "high points." They reflect the light, so any imperfections on them will really stand out.

edge; the top of the cowl; the top of the turtle deck; the sides of rounded fuselages; and the corners of square fuselages.

On a high point, bubbles, wrinkles and uneven seams are accentuated by reflected light. There's nothing difficult about doing a first-class job on these areas. It just takes some forethought and a little extra patience.

EYE POINTS
People are often careless when they cover eye points (perhaps because they're difficult to cover), so these areas usually receive the most scrutiny—

13-3. The top of the cowl is another high point where the quality of the covering job is accentuated by reflected light.

13-4. The edges of control surfaces are eye points, so they're among the places that judges will surely scrutinize.

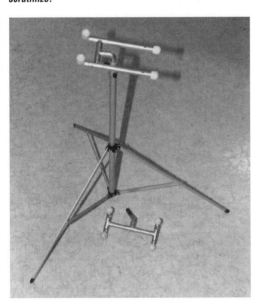

13-5. Your model will look better if you take the time to build a brace for it that can fit on top of a tripod. Two custom-made braces are shown here.

do an extra-neat job on eye points. A good covering job on these areas will certainly overshadow a little wrinkle or bubble someplace else.

WINNING CONTESTS

There aren't any steadfast rules, because static contests don't usually have set judging guidelines. Judges are people, and people have their own likes and dislikes. In addition, most static contests are open to planes with all types of finish. Often, planes that have been covered with iron-on film will compete against planes with custom paint jobs or those covered with silk and dope. I've found,

especially from judges. Eye-points include: seams under wing tips and the leading edge; seams under stab/elevator tips and the leading edge; seams on the vertical fin and the rudder; the edges and corners of all control surfaces; the joint between the stab/fin and the fuselage; the wing-root joint; the wing saddle; the edges of hatches and the cowl; hinge surfaces; fairings; and the trim or the edge around the cockpit.

It's well worth the effort to slow your pace and

13-6. The engine nacelle fairings on the Twin-Twin are eye points that attract attention.

13-7. *The Enforcerus took first place in MonoKote and second place in Sport Monoplane at the '90 Toledo show.*

made of covering material instead of trim tape.

• Insignias, numbers, names and logos made of covering material instead of decals and stick-ons.

• Sealed control surfaces on which the covering material matches the color scheme.

• A cockpit interior that has been covered with iron-on film and features details such as instruments and knobs on the dashboard.

• An aircraft that's mounted at an attractive flying attitude on a camera tripod or other stand. (See Photo 13-5.) This also allows you to angle your plane to show off its high points.

• A sign with information about the aircraft, e.g., its size/weight, the kit name and the type of covering used. It doesn't have to be elaborate (I just

however, that judges usually appreciate the following things:

• Neat work, especially on high points and eye points.

• Attractive color schemes. They don't necessarily have to be elaborate, but the colors should complement one another, e.g., red, white and blue or red, orange and yellow. Three- and four-color schemes are more attractive than simple two-color schemes.

• Two-color schemes in which thin lines of film of a contrasting color separate the two main colors.

• Scale color schemes on sport planes. A Cessna color scheme looks good on high-wing planes; military schemes look good on low-wing planes; and scale color schemes, e.g., Stinson, Pitts, etc., look good on biplanes.

• Panel lines, hatch covers and other details

13-8. *The Unitaar features flush rivets and a horn on the pilots forehead. It took first place in Sport at the '83 WRAM show.*

13-9. The Racemaster took first place in MonoKote and second place in Sport Biplane at the '91 Toledo show.

glue an $8^1/2$x11-inch sheet of paper to a piece of cardboard), but the lettering should be as large as possible. Most judges hate to take out their reading glasses to see what you've written.

ENTER CONTESTS
Have fun, and enter as many contests as you can. Don't be discouraged if you don't win them all. The things that are important to those who build models from a pile of wood aren't always the things that contest judges appreciate. Frequently, first place will go to a fiberglass jet with a professional, custom paint job. Sometimes, the judges don't seem to appreciate the work that goes into a built-up model. Sometimes, they don't care whether or not the builder did all the

work himself. Regardless of what happens, you'll know that you've given it your best shot; take pride in that. You'll receive plenty of praise—even when you don't take home a trophy.

13-10. This MiG—kit-bashed from a GP Supersportster—took third place in MonoKote and third place in Sport Monoplane at the '91 Toledo show.

Appendix

COVERING PRODUCTS

The products referred to in this book are listed below. These and a variety of other covering products are available at your local hobby dealer.

MANUFACTURER/ DISTRIBUTOR	PRODUCT
Carl Goldberg Models 4734 W. Chicago Ave Chicago, IL 60651	UltraCote Model Magic
Coverite 420 Babylon Rd. Horsham, PA 19044	21st Century Space Age Fabric 21st Century Space Age Film Black Baron Film Silkspan Micafilm Balsarite Pocket temperature gauge Heating irons/guns
Hobby Lobby International Inc. (Distributor) 5614 Franklin Pike Cir. Brentwood, TN 37027	Oracover
Hobby Shack (Distributor) 18480 Bandilier Cir. Fountain Valley, CA 92728-8610	Solartex
Micro Mark 340-1207 Snyder Ave. Berkeley Heights, NJ 07922	Tools
Sig Manufacturing Co. Inc. 401 S. Front St. Montezuma, IA 50171	Supercoat Sig Epoxolite
Top Flite Distributed by Great Planes Model Distributors P.O. Box 9021 1608 Interstate Dr. Champaign, IL 61826-9021	Super MonoKote EconoKote Heating irons/guns
Williams Bros. Inc. 181 Pawnee St. San Marcos, CA 92069	Williams Brothers Pilots